MW01152857

JAMES ISLAND

JAMES ISLAND

STORIES FROM SLAVE DESCENDANTS

EUGENE FRAZIER SR.

THE
History
PRESS

Published by The History Press
Charleston, SC 29403
www.historypress.net

Copyright © 2006 by Eugene Frazier Sr.
All rights reserved

Cover image: Photo by Jeremy Lock for *Slavery and the Making of America* broadcast by PBS.
All internal double-page spreads photographed by Deborah Silliman Wolfe in 2006 with the exception of the
photo on page 128–129, which is from the Library of Congress.

First published 2006

ISBN 978-1-5402-0435-6

Library of Congress Cataloging-in-Publication Data

Frazier, Eugene, Sr.
James Island : stories from slave descendants / [compiled by] Eugene
Frazier, Sr.
p. cm.
ISBN-13: 978-1-59629-182-9 (alk. paper)
ISBN-10: 1-59629-182-6 (alk. paper)
1. James Island (S.C.)--Social life and customs--Anecdotes. 2. Plantation
life--South Carolina--James Island--History--Anecdotes. 3. Slaves--South
Carolina--James Island--History--Anecdotes. 4. African Americans--South
Carolina--James Island--Interviews. 5. James Island
(S.C.)--Biography--Anecdotes. 6. James Island (S.C.)--Race
relations--Anecdotes. 7. African Americans--South Carolina--James
Island--Genealogy. 8. Registers of births, etc.--South Carolina--James
Island. I. Title.

F277.B3F73 2006
975.7'91--dc22
2006025849

Notice: The information in this book is true and complete to the best of our knowledge. It is offered without
guarantee on the part of the author or The History Press. The author and The History Press disclaim all
liability in connection with the use of this book.

All rights reserved. No part of this book may be reproduced or transmitted in any form whatsoever without
prior written permission from the publisher except in the case of brief quotations embodied in critical articles
and reviews.

THIS BOOK IS DEDICATED TO my great-great-grandparents, Cudjo and Mary Chavis and Benjamin and Sibby Frazier; my great-grandparents, Paul and Betsy Matthew Chavis, Jake and Violet Smalls and Cyrus and Rosa Frazier; my grandparents, Daniel and Lucy Todd Smalls and Sandy and Mary Chavis Frazier; and my parents, Sandy and Viola Smalls Frazier.

It is also dedicated to my grandmother-in-law, Hettie Gadsden Prioleau; Reverend Marion A. and Ona Belle Sanders; Mary Feedie Roper; Frank Deleston; Edna Mattie Richardson; Aida White Moore; Isaac Kinlock; Harry Urie Sr.; and all those slaves, sharecroppers and farmers who helped to pave the way in order to make this wilderness into a township called James Island; and additionally, to those who traveled on a level of time to that undiscovered country, "from who's born no traveler returns to receive their final reward that only God can give."

CONTENTS

CONTENTS

PREFACE

THIS BOOK WAS WRITTEN FOR anyone who is interested in the history of slaves on James Island. These slaves were brought from the west coast of Africa and other parts of the world to Charleston, South Carolina. The slaves of James Island struggled throughout slavery, segregation and the integration eras in order to survive and to be treated as human beings.

The book contains the names of African American slaves and their descendants that were imported to or born and raised on James Island during the slavery, sharecropping and farming era between 1732 and the 1950s. It tells of the slaves' determination during those difficult years on this small wilderness island and their relationships with plantation owners to make this island into a township.

In 1750, South Carolina had 39,000 slaves. (Source, U.S. Department of Commerce historical statistics and the Bureau of Census, Washington, D.C.) South Carolina had 107,098 slaves and 1,801 freedmen in 1790. Slaves in Charleston were sold for $500 in 1800, in 1818 for $550 and in 1837 for $1,200. (Source, Ulrich Bonnell Phillip, *The Slave Economy of the Old South*, and the Bureau of Census, Washington, D.C.)

I relied heavily on research obtained from the U.S. Census Bureau along with interviews of family members and other supporting documentation in an effort to determine the exact age of their descendants. Further, my research has uncovered some uncertainty in age as many slaves and their descendants could only guess at their ages. Many slaves did not read or write and thus left no written documentation. Therefore, family members often relied on oral history in regard to ages and birth dates. However, I investigated all possible sources, including census reports, interviews and supporting documentation, to obtain the most accurate date of birth of those listed in this book. Thus, research results and conclusions expressed are mine and have not been endorsed by the U.S. Census Bureau.

INTERVIEWS

CONVERSATIONS AND INTERVIEWS WERE HELD over the years with slaves, relatives of slaves, descendants of slaves and descendants of slave owners. During these interviews as outlined below, I am referred to by the following names: Gene, Son, Eugene and Frazier.

Names	Interview Date(s)	Lifespan
Daniel Smalls	1942 through 1953	1853–1954
Frank Deleston	1949 through 1955	1873–1956
Hettie Prioleau	1959 through 1980	1872–1986
Mary C. Frazier	1942 through 1963	1880–1963
Mary Roper	1945 through 1973	1888–1989
Livinia Gladden	1945 through 1960	1889–1961
Julia Smalls	1945 through 1947	1881–1950
Emily Champagne	1945 through 1966	1899–1968
Isaac Kinlock	1998 through 2004	1901–2006
Sandy Frazier	1940 through 1969	1908–1969
Viola S. Frazier	1940 through 1975	1908–1975
Eva F. McKelvey	1957 through 2005	1911–
Lila Lafayette	2003	1911–2004
Aida W. Moore	2001 through 2004	1914–2005
Ethel F. Campbell	1966 through 2004	1917–
Elouise S. Pinckney	2003	1914–2004
Edna R. Richardson	1995 through 2005	1914–
Kerzel Fleming	2001	1916–
Bernice Black Stewart	2004	1916–

Harry Urie	1995 through 2003	1916–2003
Jack O. White	2003	1922–
Lillian Washington	1993 through 2004	1925–
Names	Interview Date(s)	Lifespan
Charlie Goss	2002 through 2003	1927–2003
Ruby W. Bellenger	2002	1927–2004
Joe Deleston	2002 through 2004	1929–2004
Levola W. Whaley	1992 through 2003	1929–
Harold Singelton	2003 through 2004	1920–2005
Kerzel Drayton Fleming	2003 through 2004	1924–
Jeffery Lemon	1960 through 1970	1910–1984
Cecelia Simmons Green	2002 through 2004	1915–

CHARLESTON
SOUTH CAROLINA

CHARLESTON, SOUTH CAROLINA, HAS A population of more than 309,000 citizens; over 34 percent are African Americans. It sits on the East Coast along the Atlantic Ocean, between North Carolina and Georgia, and is a busy seaport city that is one of the main points of entry for industrial ships entering the states on the East Coast. It was the main point of entry for slaves entering this country during the era of slavery.

Most visitors who come in contact with Charleston seem to love her outpouring of friendliness and Southern hospitality. The city has a reputation for attracting tourists and visitors. Four of the islands in the Lowcountry, Edisto Island, Wadmalaw Island, Johns Island and James Island, are rich with African American heritage and culture.

Charleston is a small city when compared with places such as New York City and Atlanta, Georgia, but it still has all the ingredients of a big city, including a history of political cronyism.

Charleston, lined with its antebellum homes, is a beautiful sight during the summer months. However, there is a dark side to the history of Charleston in regard to race relations that many whites would rather keep hidden in the past, but the truth remains that discrimination is as prevalent today as it was decades ago, only subtler. Although some progress has been made in race relations in South Carolina since the Civil War, Charleston still lags behind most cities in reference to the economic and political advancement of African Americans.

I was born and raised on James Island and I lived through some of those difficult years of segregation and the frustrations of integration. I know what these living conditions were like for blacks. As I was writing this book, I thought about the inhuman treatment of blacks during and following slavery and the feelings of hopelessness and frustration that my ancestors must have felt as they were kidnapped from their homeland and chained aboard ships in inhumane and horrendous living conditions, only to be brought to North America to become human chattel.

Old Slave Market located on Chalmers Street in Charleston, SC. *Family photograph.*

I could only imagine the despair and fear in their hearts and minds, stacked like animals by the thousands aboard these ships in an excruciating and painful journey to this faraway land called North America. Historians report thousands of slaves died during these journeys from disease, starvation, dysentery and assaults committed against each other in order to survive. More than 40 percent of the slaves arriving from these journeys entered this country through the Port of Charleston. As ships arrived in this country on Sullivan's Island, many slaves found themselves in the South Santee area forty-five miles from Charleston. According to my grandfather, it was on the Santee plantation where my maternal great-grandfather Jake Smalls (1798), his wife Violet Smalls (1810) and many slaves ended up living. My maternal great-grandfather and his wife had ten sons and two daughters. My grandpa Daniel was the third oldest.

Grandpa Daniel Smalls (1853–1954) said his parents and many other slaves made the journey to Charleston on foot. They walked barefoot with rags wrapped around their feet, through the woods, swamps and canals. When they reached Charleston, their feet were bruised and raw with dried blood encrusted around their swollen ankles. The Massa (slave master) rode horses and wagons as the slaves walked. Some of the older slaves were blindfolded during the day as they walked to keep them from escaping.

Historical records show that slaves were auctioned at the Old Slave Market located at 6 Chalmers Street in downtown Charleston. The building is still intact

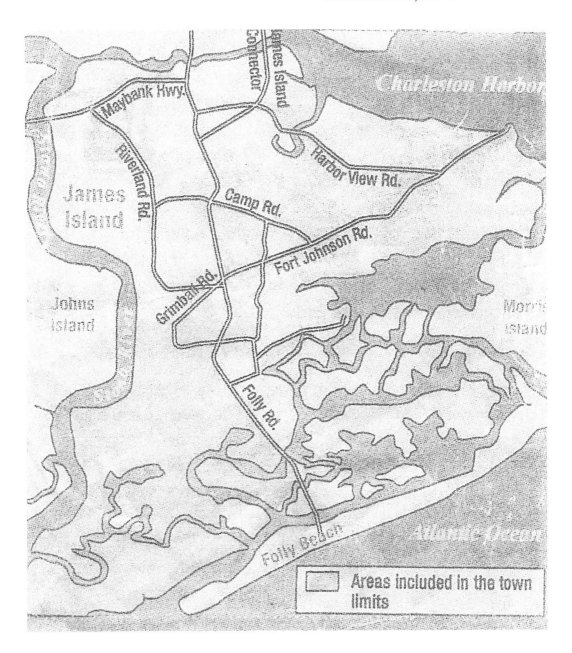

Map of the town of James Island. *Courtesy of Charleston County Library.*

First bridge across the Wappoo Creek (1899–1900). *From the collections of the SC Historical Society.*

as of this writing and sits next door to the law office of attorney Gedney Howe III. It is well preserved for historical purposes.

I had the privilege of visiting this historical building on several occasions during the late 1960s, due to my friendship with Gedney. This friendship began as a result of my employment with the Charleston County Police Department and continues to the present. I experienced an "eerie" feeling while standing inside this building where my great-grandpa, grandma and thousands of other slaves were auctioned off like cattle. Grandpa's family was sold to the Dill Plantation. They rode on a ferry from Charleston to James Island.

Records in the archives revealed that the last groups of slaves were children who were auctioned in Charleston on the corner of Ann and King Street in 1865.

What was known as the "Township of James Island" is located approximately seven miles west of downtown Charleston. It is an island surrounded by the Atlantic Ocean, Wappoo River and the Stono River. During the 1800s, the only access to and from the island was by ferry or boats. In 1899, a wooden trestle bridge was built across the Wappoo Creek that connected her to the Charleston peninsula in downtown Charleston.

There were several slave and sharecropper plantations on James Island. The first plantation starting from the Wappoo Cut Bridge was the McLeod and following were the Dill, Grimball, Rivers, Ellis, Seabrook, Clark, Lawton, Hinson, Mikell, Royall, Croskey, Lebby, Legare, Freer, Bee and Mellechamp Plantations. Some of these plantation owners were relatives and farmed the same properties, fathers, sons, sons-in-law, brothers, nephews, etc., as the properties were sold or passed down through the generations.

Hundreds of slave descendants still live on property their ancestors bought from the plantation owners during and after slavery. This information was collected, substantiated and corroborated from records obtained from archives in the Charleston County Library, County Courts, RMC Office, Columbia, and also records kept by family members of slaves, descendants of slave owners and through this writer's personal knowledge and experiences during the segregation and integration eras.

During numerous conversations over the years, and in taped interviews with many of the people, I quoted them to stay true to their dialect.

The Dill
Plantation Owners

J oseph Dill (1724–1796) and his wife Sarah (1742–1811) were the plantation owners. They had one son, Joseph T., who was married to Regina Dill. Joseph T. and Regina had one son who was also named Joseph T. (1822–1900). During his lifespan, Joseph T. married Eleanor C. Rivers Dill. He would later marry Frances Hinson and this marriage produced three daughters, Julia R., Pauline R. and Frances.

The managers and overseers of the Dill farms during the sharecropping and farming era were Fuller C. King (1879) and his wife, Mary Leize King (1885). They had two sons, Lebby B. (1909) and Marion B. (1911), and a daughter, Lillie B. (1915). Farming the plantation through the 1960s were Park Mikell (1897) and his wife, Dorothy A. Mikell (1904). They had two daughters, Dorothy A. (1923) and Francis (1925).

The slave schedule from 1850 to 1860 shows that the Dill families owned 190 slaves during this era.

The Dill house sits on the bank of the Stono River in its original position, with remodeling done to the original structure. The roadway stretches from Riverland Drive to the residence. The Dill Plantation was flanked by the Stono River, Wappoo Cut River to the north, McLeod Plantation to the east and Grimball Plantation. It traveled across Folly Road covering that area from Fort Johnson Road to Camp Road to an area behind James Island Presbyterian Church.

Slaves and Their Descendants Residing on the Dill Plantation

I recall stories that were told to me by former slaves or their descendants about the locations of their cabins beginning at the banks of the Stono River, in front of the Civil War battery and along the Stono Road where Fergerson Village now stands. Many of the inhabitants of these cabins died long before my birth but their existence and legacy lives on.

In the first cabin were Charlie Goss (1844) and his wife Betsy (1856). They had one son, Edward, and two daughters, Celia and Ida. His mother, Martha Goss

Road leading from Riverland Drive to the Dill House. *Family photograph.*

Charlie Goss. *Family photograph.*

(1820), and three grandsons, Charlie, Herman and Alonzo Moore, also resided with them. Charlie and his wife are buried in the Dill Slave Cemetery on Riverland Drive.

Following slavery, during the sharecropping and farming eras, Charlie was a foreman on the plantation. People in the community called Charlie "Yubber." He could not read or write and his speech was limited to very few words, as was the case of all slaves on the Dill Plantation. I recall one of his arms was amputated above the elbow. Charlie rode a horse on the farm during the time when I, beginning at the age of seven, started helping my mother and sisters harvest green beans and potatoes on the Dill farm.

Charlie Goss (1928–2003) and his wife, Christina (1932–1999), had five daughters, Venus, Christina, Stephanie, Althea and Dora; and three sons, Edward, Charlie Jr. and Freddie.

Charlie, the grandson of Charlie Goss, was called "Lee Lee" by people in the community. During our interviews over the course of three months, as I sat on his porch with him, he would hold his cane in his right hand with his chin resting on it. He looked up at the blue sky and said to me,

Son, dey old boy gettin tired now. From all them arthritis in da bone of mine—from dey hard woks, un cold run thou them on dey farm. My wife Tena, un me had some ups un down but we raised our chillin, un had a good life together.

Grandpa Charlie tells me, him un his mama waz grab from un island by white man, un bring to James Island by boat duin slavery. Grandpa did not know where dey come from; him un his mama waz sell to Dill's Plantation, dat wen he meet grandma Betsy, un dey got married. Grandpa says after slavery dey slaves Massa [Joseph Dill] make him a foreman on dey Plantation.

Grandpa raised my bubber Sporty [Herman], Lonzo [Alonzo Moore] un me cause our daddy gone to New York, wen we waz little to make a better life. He never come back home to stay. In them early dey, we had no stove. Grandpa use dey fire in dey chimmy to cook, un heat dey house duin wintertime. Duin farmin time we raised hogs to sell, dat damn house we live in waz no better un da stable dey mule live in. Wen it rain, water leak to dey house roof un we get wet in bed, on rainy nights we catch hell.

Son, my bubber un me wok on dey farm wen Park Mikell waz dey boss. We plow mules from sunup to sundown in dey fields. Sometime it be rainin, un dat shitten man ask, why dey hell we stop plowin. Dat goddamn Park Mikell waz a nasty cracker, un had no use for black people oter than wok da hell out yu.

One dey duin winter time in 1936, Grandma Betsy waz feedin da hogs, one of them boa hogs bite hur. Grandpa comes home to eat; we tell him wha happen to grandma. Grandpa tells Sporty un me to tied da boa; make a fire under da big cast-iron pot, boil da water till he get home.

Da evenin wen grandpa come home, Grandma Betsy say, "Charlie wha yu gonna do." Grandpa say, "Yu la me handle this ting omen, yu get back in da house. Sporty fetch me da axe." Grandpa chop da hog in da head killin it. Sporty, un me hold da

hog upside down, while grandpa cut da guts out. We put da hog in hot water un use knifes to clean it.

Grandpa slices da hog into lota pieces, rub salt in da meat to cure it un put da meat in a bag. Tells Sporty un me to dig a hole in da ground. We put a piece of tin in da hole, cloth on top da tin, un put da meat in da hole wid cloth on top it. Da ice man come on Satday grandpa buy fifty pounds of ice; chop it up wid a ice pick bury it in da hole wid da meat in summer time, till we need meat to eat, and sell.

Grandma Betsy say, "Grandpa waz runnin a machine dat run da conway [conveyer] belt; on da farm, handle cotton un corn. Grandpa waz talkin to one of him omen, un not pays tention to what he waz duin. His hand got catch in da machine un waz cut off. Wen Sporty un me waz born grandpa hand waz cut off. Cause he waz a foreman grandpa had a saddle horse to ride, da boss give him to check on da people in da field.

We called da hoses [horse] "Light foot" cause it run so fast. Grandpa only had one hand, but if we do roun ting, he wid still beat da hell out of we. Man I tell yu dat waz a mean shitten man, yu hear me! He hold we wid da nub arm roun we neck, un beat my bubber Sporty un me, wid dat whip handle til he tink it waz nuff.

Grandpa says wen he do roun ting duin slavery, da otersey [overseer] make him take of his shirt, un beat him wid da whip. He says da same ting happen wen we do roun things; grandpa did not like to talk bout slavery. He had lots of scab on his back from da beaten he got duin slavery. Grandma say grandpa got da beaten cause his head was so cussed hard, un not pay tention to da Massa.

Wen Sporty un me wok all weeks, get pay $6.50 on Friday, wen we come home grandpa call Sporty un me in da house and said, "All right, gimmie all da dad burn money." We give him all da money. Grandpa had a pouch he keeps money in. He gives my bubber un me 25 cents a piece. Grandma say, "Charlie, man don't treat them like dat, give them a little more." Grandpa give we another quarter, not a dad burn peny more, yu mine yu mout Betsy.

One Satday evenin grandpa come home late him un Grandma waz fussin. Grandpa waz drinkin moonshine whiskey. Grandma waz fussin bout grandpa messin wid oter omen. Grandpa say he loss da pouch he keeps his money in ridin da hoss. Grandma say, "See Charlie, you don't wanna give them boy's un me no money, but them omen yu mess wid took all."

Grandpa send Sporty un me to follow da hoss tracks to da footpath in dey wood to fine his money pouch. Sporty un me look, un look, til night but we couldn't fine da money pouch. Grandpa got his whip wid dat nub arm; wrap roun we neck, whip Sporty un me til he waz tired. Man dat waz a mean shitten goddamn man, yu hear me, I tink he believe we waz still in slavery!

Wen he dead we bury him in dat slaves' graveyard on Riverland Drive, wid all da oter slaves. After grandpa dead I stop wokin for Park Mikell, move off the farm, un went to wok for a well diggin company till I retire.

Charlie (Lee Lee) Goss died two months after my last interview with him.

Eddie Goss (1900) and his wife Venus had two sons, Charlie and Herman; and one daughter, Dolly. Eddie Goss migrated to New York during the 1940s and never returned to South Carolina to live. His wife, Venus, later married Elias Whaley of the Grimball Plantation after the death of Elias's first wife.

Joe Deleston (1881) and his wife Lizzy Smalls Deleston (1893–1964) had three daughters, Martha Deleston Richardson (1917), Josephine Deleston Walton (1928) and Isadora Deleston Moore (1926); and four sons, Henry (1923), Nathaniel Joe (1929), Walter and Jaycee. Joe Deleston, the son of Joseph (Joe) and Dolly Frazier Deleston, was born on the Grimball Plantation. Following his marriage to Lizzy Smalls, he moved to the Dill Plantation, where he worked on the farm until his death.

Joe Deleston Jr. (1929–2004) and his wife Martha Lemon Deleston (1929) had four sons, Nathaniel, Eugene, Toney and Andrew; and four daughters, Shirley, Susie, Carolyn and Lavitica. Joe was affectionately called "Nay" by the people in the community. During several interviews with him as he reflected over his life, I recall the many years that I knew him, which was for the majority of my life. I found him to be a quiet, honest, hardworking and lovable man, as did many who knew him.

Nay's father and my grandfather were first cousins. During several conversations, he said,

> Son I waz born un raised on da Dill's Plantation wid my sisters un bubbers. We live in one of them slave house, not fur from Stono River, near old man Charlie Goss, close to da tall Battery, next to Stono Road. Charlie waz foreman for Dill Plantation wen I was a boy. Older people called him "Yubber."
>
> My Papa dead wen I waz young, I don't member too much bout him. I use to go to Cut Bridge School by da little bridge at corner of Riverland Drive un Camp Road. It use to name Stono Road, un King Hi-Way long time ago. The school waz sittin right in da marsh off Riverland Drive; wen tide waz high, or rains, da school ground got flooded un we got wet.
>
> I stop school wen I waz fourteen yea old. Son, I try, un I try, but I just couldn't learn nottin. I never did learn to read un write. Mama ask me what I was gonna do, I tell mama, I guess get a job. Mama say if I didn't go to school I had to wok. I got a job wokin on Dill Plantation wen Park Mikell waz boss.
>
> Park put me plowin fields wid a mule, I plow fields from six clock in da mornin til dark wid lot of oter men; Lonzo [Alonzo Moore], Sonny Boy [Sanders Smalls], Sporty [Herman Goss], Charlie Goss un my far-law [father-in-law] Jeffery Lemon, he waz Park Mikell foreman. We got a hour to eat doin da dey; if we waz late gettin back to wok, Park raise hell, then cut our money on payday.
>
> Son, I waz youn un it waz hard wok, Mr. Park spec a lot of wok from me. I stop wokin for him, un went to wok for Oley Brown, a black man, you member Oley. Oley had a small farm in da place where we live now in Fergerson village, un a Mule name Mary. I take care of plowin fields for Oley Brown, bout a mont. Then one evenin Mr. Park come to we house mad, tell mama if I didn't come back to wok for

Joe Deleston. *Family photograph.*

him, everyone in da goddamn house, had to get da hell of his plantation. I went back to wok for him cause we had no place else to go.

On da weekend, after wok all da men un boys wid getters at Tucker's store to buy Johnny cake un drinks. Da store waz on da corner of Riverland Drive un Camp Road, near da school. It waz a one-story board buildin. Tucker and his family lived in the house next door. Son, I plow mule for yea for dat man, fore he let me drive tractors. Man yu know all dat time Mr. Park paid me $12.50 a week. Dat waz a dirty redneck cracker, mean as hell yu hear me! On Satday wen Mr. Park waz gone to Columbia to ballgame, he had a white man [George Taylor] drive a tractor trailer to da end of da cornfield, unhitch da trailer un leave it wid me.

I broke corn, un load trailer from sunrise to sundown by myself. After minimum wages pass, Park start payin me forty dollars a weeks. Wen Park got too old to run the farm, he bring in a man name Mr. Hill to run da farm. He plant string beans, taters, matos un corn on da farm, I wok for him lots of yea. After Hill retire, Acock took over farmin, he plants da whole ting wid matos. I waz da last person to retire from wokin on da farms.

Wen I waz a boy, yu know all them roads on James Island waz one lane un dirt. Wen it rains them roads got muddy, da cars un trucks try to pass each oter, un got bog down. A lota people got together un help push da car out da mud. Most of them people had cars waz whites, dey wid give we a nickel apiece to push them out.

I member wen yu waz wokin at da courthouse I waz call to jury duty. Da judge asks me if I could read un write. I tell him no, he let me go. Son I was not shame cause I still come a good family man and raised all my chillin the right way.

I remembered the incident. At the time, I was employed by the U.S. Marshal Service in 1993, at the Federal District Court in Charleston. Nay's appearance and demeanor impressed the judge and that caused him to inquire of me concerning Nay's education. I informed the judge that it was true and that Nay was an honorable man and would never mislead the court. The judge reluctantly excused him from jury duty and complimented him on his honesty and his demeanor.

Yu know da famous man Porgy, in da Porgy un Bess play? Dat waz my mama bubber. I didn't know him, he dead the yea I waz born. Mama tell me bout him. She says da family un oter peoples call him "Goat man." His real name waz Samuel Smalls. He waz cripple in his two legs un ride around in a cart with a goat pullin him. Some of my mama families to this day don't like what one of da sisters do—sell da right to his life. Yu know he buried right dey in Burn Church graveyard at Fort Johnson and Folly Road. Dey a tombstone in his memory.

I recall many times during the mid-1940s, as I rode around with my uncle James Smalls in his car, that he would stop by Nay's house to get his hair cut. Nay was a self-made barber and cut the hair of the men in the community for over two decades in addition to working on the farm.

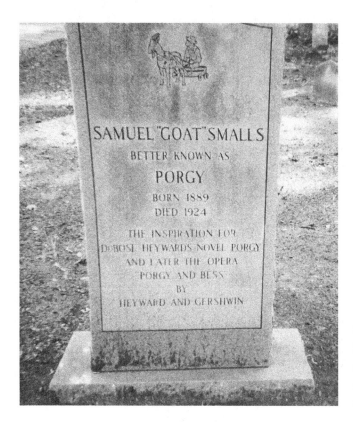

Grave of Samuel "Goat" Smalls (the inspiration for Dubose Heyward's novel *Porgy and Bess*, later made into an opera by George and Ira Gershwin). *Family photograph.*

Nay was a quiet and a humble man and one of the most respected in the community where he lived. During my last interview with Nay, his nephew Benjamin Richardson was present with us on his porch. He agrees with Nay's recollection concerning the story of Samuel Smalls (Porgy). Nay died three months following my last interview with him in 2004.

James Gladden (1836) and his wife Betsy Gadsden Gladden (1856–1931) had three sons, Louis (1874), Robert (1902) and Alonzo (1910); and three daughters, Mary (1892), Josephine (1911) and Cynthia (1913). James was one of the overseers on the Dill Plantation during slavery. They were all listed as mulattos with the exception of Betsey and Robert. Betsy Gladden died in 1931, of an apparant heart attack.

Robert Gladden (1902–1979) and his wife Elouise (1904–1969) had three sons, Herbert, William and Leroy; and three daughters, Lillian, Bernice and Agnes.

CONVERSATIONS WITH LILLIAN GLADDEN WASHINGTON

Lillian G. Washington and her husband Morris had three daughters, Barbara Ann Forest, Catherine Forest and Mary Doll Forest; and two sons Willie Forest Jr. and Morris Washington Jr.

Picture of Robert Gladden, his wife Elouise Gladden and daughter Lillian Gladden working on their farm. *Family photograph.*

Lillian, the granddaughter of James Gladden and the daughter of Robert Gladden, said,

Gene, my grandpa was an Indian. He came to James Island with a white slave owner. We lived on that section of the Dill plantation known as Fickin. That is where the Municipal Golf Course is now located on Riverland Terrace.

People used to ask my mama what that white man was doing sleeping in our house. Mama said people thought he was white. Anyway, white men could sleep with any black women and nothing was said about it. I don't have to tell you— just look at my daddy's brothers, Louis and Alonzo, and his sisters, Josephine, Cynthia and Mary, you knew them. They were all real light skinned. My grandpa was the overseer on that section of the plantation where we lives.

Gene, when I was a little girl I remembered that we lived in a small slave cabin like the one on McLeod Plantation at the corner of Folly Road and Maybank Highway. They were several of us living in that three-room cabin. The majority of the people were in the same predicament as us. I remember while I was living there, the people in the community held pray meeting on Tuesday, Thursday and Sunday nights. They worked 5½ days a week.

One Tuesday night in 1931, while the older people were having prayer meetings in Jerusalem Lodge Hall on Riverland Drive, three of us girls were listening on the outside. We thought someone inside fainted and saw people lying down on the floor. People inside were crying. One of my father's sisters, Ellen, was laughing out loud. One of the older women came outside and told her to shut up. You know that your mother is lying on the floor dead. Grandma Betsy had died of a heart attack.

The slave cabin our family lived in was old and had a leaky roof. We did not have a stove. Grandma used the fireplace in the chimney to cook and heat the house during the winter months. My father moved us to a place further south on Riverland Drive called Birchwood. This property was located in the same area where the James Island Senior Citizens Center and the Charleston County Park now stand.

Gene, the white man that leased the Birchwood property from the Dills was named Dr. McGinnis. He operated a dairy farm. He was a veterinarian. When the children were sick, he would give us aspirin and send us home. We stayed at Birchwood farm for a while, but the cabin was not much better than the one we moved out. Papa moved us from Birchwood to a house further south on Riverland Drive. Four houses were there at the time. Natty Smith lived in the first, my father in the second, David [King] Smalls in the third. Walter McMillan moved there later.

The cabins were located a short distance south of the entrance where Fergerson Village is now located. These cabins were a little better than the one we moved from. The white foreman on the plantation would come to our cabin in the morning and get us out of bed to make sure the family was on the farm even though slavery had been abolished long ago and this was the farming era.

The working condition was bad. Then one day in 1932, my maternal grandpa, Daniel Chisolm, came to our cabin. He said to Papa, "Charlie (that was his nickname), Charlie, you too smart a young man to be on a plantation. You need to get off. I bought some property from the Grimballs. I am going to give you a piece for your family."

After papa moved us from the Dill Plantation to the Grimball Plantation things were a lot better. I started working on the Grimball Plantation, planting, and pulling onions, cutting collard greens and breaking off corn from the stalks. The Grimballs treated the black people a lot better than the Dills.

Papa got a job working with Johnny Adams building the Municipal Golf Course in 1932. He helped build the golf course and the traps and bunkers for the City of Charleston. Mama got a job with papa pulling weeds from the course and planted grass on her knees in the summer and in the winter months. Gene, they were paid one dollar and fifty cent a week. It was a shame the way our parents were treated.

One summer day mama came home from work shaking and trembling. "Thank God" she kept repeating, over and over again. She said she was sitting on the ground pulling weeds, when she drifted off to sleep. She felt what she thought was like a cold belt around her neck. She jerked the thing from around her neck, and discovered it was a snake. Gene, she continued to give God thanks for the rest of her life.

During the early 1930s, Mr. Harold McGinnis was the manager of the cigar factory [American Tobacco Company]. He used to play golf at the Municipal

Golf Course. He saw my mama on her knees pulling weeds one day. He asked my papa and mama if they wanted a job working for him at the cigar factory. They said yes. Both went to work for Mr. McGinnis at the American Tobacco Company where they worked until they retired.

Even though papa and mama worked at the Municipal Golf Course and later the cigar factory, after they got off from work, they would still work on our farm until late in the evening planting, harvesting and selling vegetables to help us survive. Everyone in the family was expected to work on the farm. Papa or Mama would take the vegetables to the Charleston Market where it would be sold.

There were no high schools on James Island for blacks. After I finished middle school, I went to Burke High School in the City of Charleston. Getting a ride to school in the morning was almost impossible. The State of South Carolina did not furnish school buses for blacks during that time. They were very few black men with cars at the time. We had to walk to school. I dropped out and got a job at the cigar factory with Papa and Mama in 1943 and worked there until 1964 when I retired.

In 1965, I went to nursing school. At the time the school was located by the old rice mill where the Charleston Marina is now. After I completed my training, I worked at the Medical College Hospital until I retired in 1978. As you know I am an active member in St. James Presbyterian Church and serve as a deacon and a division leader.

Gene, I know you remember my papa and mama. He and your daddy were friends. Papa used to visit your daddy all the time besides, we all are cousins in one way or the other. Your grandma, Mary Frazier, was my class leader in St. James Presbyterian Church. Papa was a deacon and made sure all of the children went to Sunday school and church. That was the way everyone on James Island was raised in those days. We made it through life by praying, believing in God, hard work and helping each other.

Thomas Chavis (1865) and his wife Charlotte (1867) had two sons, Hezekiah (1896) and Esau (1904); and two daughters, Ernestine Chavis Picard (1897) and Sarah Chavis (1901); all were mulattos. Thomas was the son of my great-great-grandfather, Cadjoe Chavis. Thomas and his family were sharecroppers on the Dill Plantation.

Although no written record could be located, according to daughter Ernestine Chavis Picard, as told to my aunt, Ethel F. Campbell, Thomas Chavis was among the first preachers at Bethel Church at Cut Bridge when it was first organized and built.

Turkey Pen/Cut Bridge Section

Hundreds of slaves lived on that section of the Dill Plantation called Turkey Pen and Cut Bridge. Turkey Pen was located between Folly Road and Riverland Drive and bound to the north by Fergerson Village. The cabins were built along the edge of the woods and lined up in rows.

It stretched from Riverland Drive, where the Meridian subdivision is now located, eastward to Folly Road, where the Queenboro subdivision sits at the end of Turkey

Pen. The cabins had one door and two windows made of boards that swung outward. They resembled the slave cabins that presently sit on the McLeod Plantation at Maybank Highway and Folly Road. Many of the cabins were torn down during the 1940s. The rest of the cabins, including the cabin where my grandpa lived, were torn down during the late 1950s.

Among the slaves in the first row of cabins were my maternal great-grandfather and great-grandmother, Jake (Jacob) Smalls (1798) and Violet Smalls (1810). They had ten sons: Daniel, Jonas, Isaac, Cesar, Jake Jr., Thomas, Henry, Frank and Pompey; and two daughters, Mitilda and Estelle. Also living with the family was Hannah Wilson (1853).

CONVERSATIONS WITH DANIEL SMALLS

Daniel Smalls (1853–1954) and his wife Lucy Todd (1858–1940) had two daughters, Etta Smalls Urie and Viola Smalls Frazier; and one son, James Smalls. I recalled visiting my grandparents on Turkey Pen with my mother, Viola Smalls Frazier, on numerous occasions.

My earliest memory was when I was five years old during the winter months. It was cold and Grandpa had no stove. He used the fireplace in his chimney to heat the house and cook their foods. The family used kerosene oil lamps with a piece of cloth as a wick to see at night. Whenever Grandpa needed an outside light, he would use a soda bottle filled with kerosene and push a lighted cloth in the neck of the bottle. Grandpa called the light a "flambo."

I had numerous conversations with Grandpa concerning slavery and his life over the years. As I recalled, he seemed troubled when the subject came up and hardly wanted to talk about it. Over the years he told me,

> *Pa un Ma, ded afa da gu fee.* [My father and mother died after they were set free.]
> *I waz gab by Massa ot cutin fel tu dibe hum won un hos un bugy, un tok chillin tu tool un be da yed un huss boy.* [I was picked by slave master Joseph Dill, out of the cotton field, to drive him around the plantation in a horse and carriage and drive his children to and from school and be the yard and houseboy.]
> *Me bubber Jak un Joniss, wuk wit ha un shoul roun da fel un keen da dit, tu mic woter run tu the grun.* [My brothers, Jake and Jonas, used hoe and shovel to clean the ditches in the fields so water could run through the field.] *Me bubber Sesis waz wod cut fur Massa, un bul da ting fu dem.* [My brother Cesar was the carpenter for the plantation and built everything for them.]
> *Me utter bubber, pow da mule, chop da gass, ron da cutin wit uter mon un omen in da fel.* [My other brothers plowed with the mules, cleaned the grass around the cotton with other men and women in the field.] *Wen tim com tu geter da cutin, da sav tut da sac tu da cat, da mule hull um tu Massa shud.*

[When time came to pick the cotton, the slaves would carry the bag to the wagon to be hauled by mule to the storage shed.]

Da Massa gru cutin, con, wice un tata un som of da fam. [The Massa grew cotton, corn, potatoes and rice on some of the plantations.] *Me bubber Fank, wuk un da diri fam, fed un woter cow un oter ting.* [My brother Frank worked on the dairy farm. He fed, watered and milked the cows and did other work.] *Un da Fank, no gu wuk, Massa gut hum ot bid, otersey geb hum tun chop wid yip.* [One day my brother Frank did not go to work. The Massa got him out of bed and the overseer gave him ten lashes with the whip.]

Foe me gut mavid, uter go to udda fam tuk ta Lizbit Fed, but marvid Lute Tud. [Before I got married I used to go to the other farms and talk to Elizabeth Fell, but I married Lucy Todd.] *Me bin yu lon tim toger com matin wit gun.* [I've been here a long time; soldiers came marching with guns (during the Civil War).]

Grandpa could not read or write; slaves were not allowed to read and write on the Dill Plantation. He never learned. The slave cabin where my grandpa lived was still intact until the late 1950s. During the sharecropping and farming era, Grandpa said he bought a mule, a cultivator and a plow from the slave owner, Joseph Dill. He grew cabbages, corn, okra, peas, turnips, collard greens, string beans and potatoes on the property the Dills allowed him to farm. He also grew strawberries and had several plum bushes, peach and fig trees in his yard. They were still intact during the 1950s.

I remember watching Grandpa as he cut the small oak trees that he dragged out of the woods into firewood. He was a small man in stature, but strong, with a big heart. Later, I would wonder how he could work all day on the various farms and then come home in the evening and chop firewood until it was dark. I would listen to him as he talked and sang to himself in his mumbling short and raspy Gullah voice. He would place a log across a tree stump, chop it in half as he groaned and sang his favorite song, "Go Don Motis Way Don in Egypt Lan" ("Go Down Moses, Way Down in Egypt Land").

I watched as Grandpa, Grandma and many people during the farming era grew old working on the farms from sunrise to sundown. I wondered what made them persevere through the hardships, frustrations and helplessness without ever complaining. In retrospect, I already knew the answer. It seemed that their belief in God was what allowed them to survive those trials, tribulations, suffering and misery. Many times I heard them saying, "God can make a way out of no way." During those years, many of the households I visited had a Bible. Most people could not read or write, yet many were able to quote verses from the Bible.

They had those deep spiritual feelings that reached down in the inner soul that would tell of the hurt and suffering as they sang. They sang those old gospel songs that only the Negro could sing with such deep feelings that only black folks understood. Songs such as "Amazing Grace," "Nobody Knows the Trouble I See," "Mary Don't You Weep Don't You Moan," "I Want Jesus to Walk With Me" and "Go Down Moses Way Down in Egypt Land," just to name a few.

Canal that runs through the Dill Plantation. *Family photograph.*

To understand the depth of this feeling, I believe you would have to have heard the late and great gospel singers like Mahalia Jackson, James Cleveland, Ray Charles and the gospel and blues singer Sam Cooke. Their voices would take you to a level of euphoria that seemed as though you never wanted them to quit.

Across the small trail on the south side, about five hundred yards in front of Grandpa's cabin, stood several cabins lined in a row. The trail that separated the property line was wide enough for a mule and wagon to pass through. As I walked with Grandpa down the trail, he pointed to several cabins. He said, "Wen oder sav ded yon um tay un da huss." (When older slave die young one stay in the house.)

Many times when I visited my grandpa in Turkey Pen, my mother would send me down the footpath to Uncle Cesar's house to cut some firewood for him. He was getting old and his only son had been killed in World War II. After his death, Uncle Cesar was buried in St. James Presbyterian Church's cemetery.

When I was about six years old, there were no roads that ran directly from the Dill Plantation in Turkey Pen to the Grimball Plantation. My father, mother and paternal grandparents lived on the Grimball Plantation some three miles away. My maternal grandpa, Daniel Smalls, would take me walking with him on numerous occasions when I slept over. In order to reach the Grimball Plantation, we had to walk across open fields, through footpaths and a trail that ran through dense woods and across a small canal.

Grandpa would place me over his shoulders with my legs straddled around his neck. He would use a long piece of oak pole for balance and tell me "ho un" (hold on). He would wade through water that sometimes reached to his shoulder, depending on the tide. There was a rope tied to a bush that stretched across the small canal on the opposite side to keep people from drowning.

This canal ran from the Stono River, under Riverland Drive, through the Dill Plantation to Folly Road and adjacent to where the First Federal Bank and Wal-Mart stores now stand. It traveled east under Folly Road, and followed a path across the island that ultimately empties into the Ashley River.

After crossing this canal, there were more dense woods and open fields to cross before reaching Riverland Drive. At this point, there was an open entrance between the tall battery for people and traffic to pass through near the slave cabin where Jeffery Lemon and his family once lived.

Still there were other times when I would walk with Grandpa along the winding road (Riverland Drive), from that section known as Cut Bridge and where Fergerson Village now stands. As we walked along the sand surface of the unpaved road headed toward Grimball Road, I would gaze at the huge tall oaks trees that lined both sides of the small road.

Some of the trees overlapped high above the road and created shade from the hot sun. As my grandfather and I walked on the small dirt road, we avoided going across the canal. Occasionally we would step off the road into the bushes, out of the way of passing trucks, farm tractors and mules pulling wagons.

As we walked along the road, the moss would sometimes fall from trees high above us to the ground. As my bare feet sank into the moss on the sand surface of the dirt road, we passed an entrance to a big house. This house was about 1,500 yards down a long dirt road that ended at the Stono River.

My grandpa told me that was the house where the Dills and the Kings once lived. In fact, the house still stands on the Dill Plantation to this day and until recently was kept by the caretaker, William Cribb. (Mr. Cribb is now retired.) Most of the trees are still intact on that section of Riverland Drive to this day.

Just one hundred yards farther south on Riverland Drive, on the south side into this wooded area, is the old Stono slave cemetery (Dill Cemetery). There my grandpa stood for a moment, looking at the cemetery with an affectionate but sad look on his face. I would learn later this was the place his wife (Grandma Lucy), my sister Lydia and my brother Sandy Jr., were all buried.

On several occasions, Grandpa and I would visit his two brothers-in-law, Primus Todd and Joe Todd (Grandma Lucy's brothers). The area where they lived was lowland and flooded when it rained. It was east of Folly Road in McColl wooded area, where Pauline Drive is now located.

There was one occasion when I walked with Grandpa to the tall battery. He began telling me, "Pa say sav dig the dit wit shual un pie thm hi up." (His father said slaves dig

William Cribb standing by an airplane hangar at the Carolina Sky Way Airport. *Family photograph.*

The battery. *Family photograph.*

the dirt for the battery with shovels and piled the dirt up high.) During this occasion, he pointed out a cannonball left behind by Confederate soldiers who defended Charleston during the Civil War.

However, at the time I was too young to appreciate the significant part of that history. In fact, one of those cannonballs exploded and killed a local farmer's son, George Nungezer Jr., a teenager (1933–1948). He was beating on the cannonball with a hammer in the Fort Johnson area of James Island when it exploded and killed him.

During this time, my father was working on the Nungezer farm. I vividly remember him coming home breaking the news concerning little George's death. Evidently, little George used to follow my father around on the farm and became attached to him. He was the only child of George Nungezer Sr.

Approximately 150 yards to the west was the entrance to the Carolina Sky Way Airport. This airport was used by Citadel cadets during World War II for flying lessons. Just fifty yards to the east on Riverland Drive was the old Negro building, the King Solomon Lodge Hall where the farmers' mill was located. This was where they would grind their corn to make grits and batter the hulls from their rice during the sharecropping and farming era.

The people used this entrance as a footpath to cross the land owned by my grandaunt, Mary Duxien Todd, and the land owned by Paul Chisolm. This was a shortcut to reach the Grimball Plantation. Otherwise they would have to walk Riverland Drive to where it intersects with Grimball Road to avoid the dense woods. In fact, King Solomon Lodge Hall still stands on Riverland Drive as a landmark to this day.

One of my lasting memories of my grandpa occurred the week before I left for my enlistment in the United States Army. My mother and I were visiting him at my Aunt Etta's house on Turkey Pen. My mother told Grandpa that I was leaving in a week to join the army.

He looked at me with an expression of happiness and joy. This was a look that I had seen on many occasions when he and I walked together over the years. He shook my hand, patted me on the back, hugged me, looked at my mother and said in his Gullah language, "Tol yu hum mak som ting gud out hum sef." (Told you he going to make something good out of himself.)

My grandpa was unusual in his demonstrations of affection, as very few black men on James Island believed in giving hugs and pats during those times—especially to young people. This was one of the things that endeared me to him.

Grandpa was ninety-nine years old at that time, and he was still walking around in the community. He was a strong man both physically and mentally. I was really hurt when I received the message a year later, in 1954, that he had died. I was stationed in Korea and requested to attend his funeral. However, due to the army's policy that funeral requests would only be granted for close relatives such as mothers and fathers, I was denied my request and thus unable to attend the funeral of my grandfather, who was also my mentor, my friend and in many ways my champion. I don't think I understood it then but I do now. For you see, my grandfather lived in a time and a place where few would have survived in the manner that he did. He survived with dignity, with determination and with love. He knew the importance of love and showed it through his hugs, his pats and his friendship even though there must have been many times in his life when he felt unloved.

Slaves and their families had little time for demonstrations of love. Their lives were governed by work and by the time they returned to their cabins, they were too fatigued to think about demonstrations of love to their children. Yet somehow, my grandfather understood the importance of it in my life. He became a source of inspiration for me. I loved my grandfather and with each passing year, I cherish my memories of him. He will forever occupy a special place in my heart.

OTHER OCCUPANTS OF SLAVE CABINS ON THE DILL PLANTATION

William Champagne (1842) and his wife Rebecca (1845) had two daughters, Emma (1868) and Alice. His mother, Amy (1793), also lived with them.

Fredrick (Cuffie) Champagne (1870) and his wife Emma (1868–1946) had two daughters, Mary (1888) and Alice (1890); one son, Fredrick Jr. (1899); a stepson, Augusta (1918); and an adopted daughter, Emily Singelton (1912). After the death of Fredrick Champagne, Emma married Murray Brown (1872). I remember Ms. Emma. She had pears and fig trees in her yard just as my grandfather had.

Grave of Daniel Smalls, author's maternal grandfather (1853–1954). *Family photograph.*

King Solomon Lodge located on Riverland Drive (2005). *Family photograph.*

I remember one particular Sunday in the summer of 1946. Ms. Emma was visiting her daughter, Mary Champagne Roper, who by now was married and lived on the Grimball Plantation. Many times as she passed our house on her way to visit her daughter, she would stop and talk with my mother and father. There was a shortcut through the woods on a trail that ran behind the Frazier and Deleston property, about a mile from where her daughter lived in the Barnhill section of the Grimball Plantation.

She was walking through the woods that Sunday morning going to her daughter's house, but later that evening, someone found her body on the footpath dead. She had died of an apparent heart attack. I remember her as a very nice, quiet, compassionate woman. She always had something good to say when she met you. I still remember her beautiful long, gray hair that shone like silver.

John Kinlock (1876) and his wife Lucy (1878) had three sons, Isaac (1901), Benjamin (1907) and Joseph (1909); and two daughters, Evelyna (1904) and Clorissia (1905).

Isaac Kinlock (1901–2006) and his wife Mary (1903) had two sons, Thomas and William; and two daughters, Florence and Dorothy; and Isaac's brother who lived with them, Ben. During several interviews with Isaac Kinlock, as I talked with him, I could not help but feel as though I was being drawn back in time through those difficult years in his life. He said,

> *Son, I waz born and raised on Dill Plantation, just like my Papa, Mama, Grandpa and Grandma. I waz youn wen they dead.*
>
> *I member your grandpa Dan Smalls, he waz Dill's and King's private chauffeur, drivin a horse and buggy take Dill's chillin to school, and wok in dey house and yard. Your uncle Cesar Smalls waz carpenter for dey plantation. I member a lot of old man and youn men wokin on dey plantation: Charlie Goss, Franklin Gilliard, King Smalls, Son Bennett [James Bennett], Fred Champagne, Hump Urie, Jonas Sanders, Willie Sanders, your grandpa bubbers and a lot more.*
>
> *Dat big bell by Dill's house rings ever mornin at daybreak wakin up dey peoples. Some wake by rooster crowing. We had thirty minute to fix some ting to eat, fry bread with molasses and sweet water tea. Mama use lard to fry the bread, you all called it pancake now. Dey second time dey bell ring we had to be at dey storage shed next to Dill's house. Dat where dey otersey wid give we our job. Plowin the mule, diggin trench thou dey fields wid shovel so water could wet dey plants, pick cotton, dig potatoes, depend on what season it waz.*
>
> *I wok on dey farms from time I waz a young boy, six years old, pickin cotton and diggin potatoes. We use pitch fork and rake to dig potatoes. Wen I got older, Mr. King starts lettin me plow dey field wid a mule. Duin da dey we had a hour to eat and get back to dey Cut Bridge sections of Dill Plantation fields. We wok until dey sun goes down, cool them mule down and water them fore beddin them down in dey stable for dey night.*
>
> *Wen cotton waz ready to be pick of dey bush, we wid tie crocker sacks around we waist then walk down them long rows pickin dey cotton. Dey bag hold bout ten pound full, touchin da ground as you walk along. Son, I tell you dat waz hard wok bendin over all day pickin cotton. Dey old people usta sing them old Negro song all day long*

while dey wok and pray. Wen dey sack waz full, we carry dey cotton to end of dey field and dump it in a bundle.

We did dey same ting breakin corn from dey stocks; carry it in crocker sack, or a wire basket to end of dey field. Wen I got fifteen year old Mr. King starts payin me fifty cent a week. Dey women and chillin's waz pay one cent a pound pickin cotton. I member old man Charlie Goss, he waz a foreman on dey plantation. Charlie, Miss Sarah [Sarah Fell] and your Grandpa waz dey oldest livin slaves duin dey time. Charlie acted like he own dey damn plantation; he ride a saddle horse [Palomino] checkin dey wokers in dey fields while we pick cotton, potatoes and string beans and do oter wok on dey farm. Wen I waz youn I use ta watch him ride his horse. It dance sideways and trot. He waz a small man, but man he could be mean "arrogant" sometime cuss like a darn sailor. Dey older people call him by his nickname. Wen dey see him comin dey wid say here come "Yubber," cowboy Charlie, as dey horse dance sideway.

Dey omen wokin on dey farms use to whisper bout Charlie and his horse visitin oter omen house at night. Charlie wid drink his moonshine whiskey out a half-pint plastic flask he carried in his back pant pocket, he wid flash his money to temp dey omen. It waz dark at night on dey island most land was woods and bushes. It waz like a wilderness. Son, a lota a ting happen after dark in them woods, if you know what I mean, dat why you have a lot of half white chillins on James Island.

Mr. Kinlock looked at me out the corner of his eyes with a grin on his face; I knew what he meant.

Wen Charlie got tight he wid climb on his horse and dat stallion wid take him home. I member one mornin Charlie was runnin dey cotton machine, talkin, not pay tention to what he duin. His shirtsleeves got catch in dey machine and one of his hands had to be cut off.

Mr. King waz runnin dey plantation duin dey time, offer to build Charlie a house way from the place where he lives, to another part of dey farm where dat shoppin center build at Folly Road and Riverland Drive is now; but Charlie want to stay on dey plantation where he lives. Charlie say no and Mr. King let Charlie stay in his slave house till he dead. Boy, I member yu Uncle Cesar tell Charlie, man you is a damn fool.

Son, dey old man tell me duin slavery, dey had to use axe, grubbin hoe make of steel and metal diggin up trees, roots, tunin dey sand up, clearin dey bushes, trees and vines wid bush knife for Dill to farm dey land. We waz still duin dey same ting in 1910, wen I waz a boy. Son, I tell yu dat waz tough time wokin in the cold, hot, sun and rain. I waz born in 1901, your grandpa and all them oter man waz old when I waz born. Dey knows all bout slavery. I use to wonder how dey makes it thru slavery. Man I caught hell, so I could margin dey hell dey catch, but dey made the best of what dey had with pray and believe in God.

All them yea, I never forgot the look on otersey King face wen he got mad, he calls any black people roun him a goddamn nigger. Dey only black man I know waz not scared of Mr. King waz Son Bennett [James Bennett]. Some time I wonder if he cares weter he live or dead, dat waz one shitten man wen he got mad. Son Bennett say he did not give a damn about any white man cause dey way dey treat his Pa and Ma duin slavery, say he might as well kill one of them s.o.b before dey killed him.

Wen I was a boy and peoples got sick, I member dey old people goin in dey wood; dig up certun kind of roots from the trees. Dey boil them, and make medicine for dey family wen dey waz sick. If dey medicine did not get them well, dey people wid go to Grimball Plantation, dat where your great-grandpa, Cyrus Frazier, waz dey doctor on James Island. People wid sometime stay at his house for deys til dey get well.

I wok on dey farm until I was about twenty-five years old before I stop. I got a job wokin for a man called Mr. Nick, drivin tractor, scrapin and repain dey roads on James Island. Duin dey time Mr. Nick waz in charge of all dey roads on James Island for dey County. I member some of dey men wokin wid me, Bennie Gladden, Louis Gladden, St. June [Joseph Deleston] and some names I forgot now.

Wen I got off from wok, I wid wok on my small farm, me and my family wid plant and grow vegetable to help make end meet. I had a small truck and took my vegetables to Charleston to sell on dey market. Some time I wid drive round in town and to people house on dey island to sell my vegetables. Son I am blessed. God help me to live to be 104 years old.

Isaac Kinlock was a member of St. James Presbyterian Church. My interviews with him took place in January, March and September of 1999 through 2005. I was amazed at his complete control of his faculties at age 104. Unfortunately, Issac Kinlock died early in 2006, never fully knowing how invaluable his contribution would be to the publication of this book dedicated to preserving his memory and the memories of those other founding fathers and mothers of James Island.

Daniel Fell (1823) was married to Sarah (1830–1934). Others residing in the household included Bella Brown (1861), Julia Washington (1854), Betsy Washington (1847) and William Washington (1868). After the death of Daniel, Sarah married James Washington.

Hump Urie Sr. (1844) and his wife Miley (1854) had two sons, Hump Jr. and Elias; and three daughters, Janie, Julia and Elouise. Miley Urie was an Indian and lived on Kiawah Island. She was kidnapped from an Indian festival, held at the place now known as Angel Oak on Johns Island, and sold to the Dill Plantation, where she met and married Hump Urie (as told to her grandson Harry Urie).

Joseph Gadsden (1894) and his wife Janie Urie (1896) had five sons, Harry Urie, Robert Gadsden, John Gadsden, Joseph Gadsden Jr. and Sidney Gadsden; and two daughters, Estelle Gadsden and Julia Gadsden.

Harry Urie (1916–2002), and his wife Florence Champaign (1923) had six sons, Harry, Glen, Elias L., Samuel, Keith C. and Bernard; and six daughters, Evelyn, Irene, Kathleen, Janie, Kate S. and Terri. Harry Urie is listed as a mulatto.

During several interviews with Harry Urie, over the years, I sat in his front room at his home in Fergerson Village. As he reflected back over his life, with

Miley Urie. *Family photograph.*

Harry Urie. *Family photograph.*

his head resting on his walking cane held in his hand, I could not help being overwhelmed by this man and the vast knowledge he possessed of African American history on James Island. Harry said,

I am telling you what I know and was taught concerning slavery, sharecropping and farming time growing up. I don't think the white man will ever tell the whole truth about slavery on James Island. The ways our people were treated without it being slanted from their point of views I want you to write what I know, and what I was taught.

My grandpa, Hump, told me that he was born in Portugal; he was a young boy working on boats and was a slave. He remembered his mother and father taken by white men, but he never knew where, or who his mother and father were sold to. The white men came one day and took them away as he hide behind some bushes. He decided to run away got on a boat and became a store away. During the trip, a lot of slaves that died were thrown overboard. He ate what he could find without getting caught. When the boat finally docked, he got off the boat and found himself in what is now known as Mt. Pleasant.

A white man caught him and asked for his freedmen paper. Slaves that were freed in South Carolina had to travel with their papers. My grandpa did not have one. The man told him you belong to me. The white man took my grandpa to the slave market in Charleston on Chalmers Street. He was sold to McLeod Plantation. McLeod sold him to the Dill Plantation where he met my grandma.

My grandma, Miley Urie, was an Indian and lived on Kiawah Island. She told me several family members were attending an Indian festival at the place now known as Angel Oak on Johns Island. Her mother, two sisters and she were kidnapped by white men. She was sold to the Dill Plantation, where she met and married my grandpa. Look at her picture, you can tell she is definitely an Indian.

Grandma Miley said her sisters and mother were screaming, kicking and fighting as they were separated, taken and sold to different plantation. Grandma was always sad when she talked about her mother and sisters, said she never saw them again, or found out where or what plantation they were sold to. She kept looking and hoping but never did find them before she died.

Grandpa and Grandma had three daughters, Janie Urie, my mother, Julia Urie, and Elouise Urie, two sons, Hump Urie Jr. and Elias Urie. We lived in one of the slaves cabins next to the canal that flows through the plantations. My uncle Hump married Etta Smalls. My mother, Janie, married Joseph Gadsden, my stepfather. I was born before they were married my stepfather was a captain on a large boat that hauls freight for the Dills, McLeods and the Grimballs.

After my uncle Hump and Etta got married, they moved into one of the slave cabins near the canal. Hump never did like working on the farm. He said it remind him of being a slave. Hump would always say he don't like the way them "goddamn crackers treated his parents." Hump got a job working at the fertilizer plant in North Charleston during the winter months in the 1920s.

At the end of the farming season during the winter months, the men on the plantations were allowed to work on other jobs off the plantations. As soon as

planting season came, they had to return to the farm. If they didn't, that family had to move off the plantation.

Hump refused to return during the farming season. Mr. King sent Thomas Middleton, a black constable to tell Hump he had to come back to work or get off the plantation. Hump told Middleton he was not working on any goddamn farm anymore. Mr. King decided to let them stay after his wife Etta was still farming and she had help from her three sons.

The Dills would furnish the seeds for the farmers to plant and harvest the crop. They had to sell their vegetables to the Dill Plantation during the early years of sharecropping. The farmer would be paid whatever amount the Dills thought the vegetables were worth minus the rent and seeds.

I remember that large bell about ten feet high in the yard by the Dills' house. In the morning as soon as it was daybreak, the first bell would ring. This tells the people it was time to get up. Thirty minutes later the second bell would ring. That meant they better start running to work because they only had thirty minutes to reach the yard. It was located by the Dills' house next to the Stono River. The bell was still there in 1953.

When the bell rings the third time, each foreman would have a crew and head to their assigned fields. Grandpa said if you were late, you get a chop from a whip for every minute you were late during slavery by the overseer. One morning Grandpa said one of the women from the Brown family that lived next door to them was late getting to the field because she was sick.

He tried to help her and told the overseer the reason he was late. The overseer got angry with him and gave him five lashes with a whip in her place and told him he was not a goddamn doctor. Grandma Miley had to put leaves and barks from a tree to heal the wounds over his body.

The Dills' house is close to the Stono River. There was a tunnel that ran underneath the house toward the river. Several times I went inside the tunnel with the older men. They told me the tunnel was built before the Civil War. The slave owner could hide from the Yankee soldier. I was also in the tunnel under the two-story house at McLeod Plantation. Grandpa said the house was also used as a hospital for Confederate soldiers during the Civil War.

This account of Hump Urie, as told to his grandson Harry, states that Confederate soldiers once used the McLeod house as a hospital and that it was also occupied by the solders of the black Fifty-fourth Regiment. This is well documented in history books written about the Fifty-fourth Regiment from Massachusetts, which fought on James Island during the Civil War. Harry continued,

I remember your grandpa, Daniel Smalls; he used to drive Mr. King around the Dill Plantation in their horse and buggy. He use to drive the Dill children to school in the City of Charleston. There was a wooden bridge across the Wappoo River in front of McLeod Plantation near where the Country Club Golf Course is now.

Do you remember that hot summer's day in 1946 when Pauline Dill chauffeur drove her to Hump and Etta house? Your grandpa was there. Etta nickname was "Child." Your mother nickname was "Sis." You and your mother, Sis, was there. Your grandpa kept the graves of the Dill family clean in the cemetery at St. James Episcopal Church on Camp Road from slavery until a few years before he died; Pauline came by to give him some money.

Did you remember when Pauline asked your grandpa how old he was? He did not know. Pauline asks him what was the oldest thing he could remember on the plantation. In his Gullah voice, your grandpa said he was a young boy picking cotton for a long time. He remembers soldiers on the island with their gun. He told her years later, "I was picked by your father to drive him around in the horse and buggy and take you and Julia to school."

After Pauline did some figuring, she said Daniel, "Although we knew you were the oldest living slave on the plantation, you realize you are over ninety years old!" Your mother, Sis, said Pauline visited your grandpa until the year before he died. Your grandpa was a physical strong man; he walks around, and was active until about three months before he died. [I remembered when Pauline Dill came to visit my grandfather.]

Your uncle Cesar was the carpenter for the plantation. I remember the first time I saw a wooden coffin. My aunt, Etta, and your mother, Sis, had infant sons died. Cesar built the coffin for them. During those days, if someone on the plantation dies, the Dills would give that family enough lumber for your uncle Cesar to build them a coffin. Across the small road in front of your grandpa house lives Ms. Emma Champagne. Her husband died when I was a young boy. She had two daughters Mary and Alice, and a son Augusta Champagne, we use to play together.

Ms. Emma raised an adopted daughter named Emily Singelton, we called her "Cord." Your mother and Cord were friends. They use to play and go to school together. They were beautiful black women. Cord got married to Joseph Deleston Sr., and your mother married your father, Sandy Frazier Jr. People called your daddy Boise and Joseph, St. June.

During the Christmas seasons, the Dill daughters, Pauline and Julia, would visit the children gathered on the plantation at your grandpa house. They would give each of the children a Mary Jane, a jawbone breaker candy that sells two for one cent for Christmas. Could you believe that shit? How stingy the Dill people were? All the money they made of our poor people sweat and brows and gave us children two piece of candy for Christmas!

You know that place called Queenboro off Folly Road. During slavery and sharecrop time, Grandpa Hump said that place was known as McColl Wood. The Dills had dozens of slave cabins there. It was located on the east side of Folly Road, in the area where Pauline Drive is now located behind James Island white Presbyterian church. Your granduncle Primus and Joe Todd and several others slaves and sharecrop families' lives there. All the property over there was wooded or farmland except where the slave cabins was built.

Your grandaunt, name was Ms. Mary Todd, but we called her Ms. Lilly. She was married to Primus Todd. They used to live in McColl woods, before moving to the house on Riverland Drive, by King Solomon Lodge Hall, after the death of her husband. During slavery and sharecrop time, grandpa said there was at one time over three hundred slaves on the Dill plantation in four difference section on the islands.

I am going to tell you this, but I know you already know. My father's name was Edward L. "Neddie" Grimball. He was a white man and cousin to the Grimballs off the Grimball Plantation on James Island. He lived on the Johns Island side of the Stono River across from the Grimball Plantation near the place known as Exchange Landing.

My mother told me while she was working for the family, Edward L. "Neddie" Grimball had sex with her. She was a young woman when she got pregnant and I was born. She said if a white man wanted to have sex with black women during those days, they was nothing the women could do about it. After I was born she married my stepfather, Joseph Gadsden.

She told me Neddie Grimball help Joseph get the job as a boat captain hauling freight for the Grimballs and the Dills. My stepfather would haul the people in the big ferry boat, beginning at the Exchange dock on Johns Island, then pickup peoples at the Grimball's, Dill's, McLeod's and Seabrook's docks on the Stono River; traveling down the Ashley River to Charleston. This was their only mean of transportations before the bridges were built.

The Grimballs had the contract to haul all the vegetables from the different plantations on the islands to Charleston. They had two boats; one was called the Seminoles. Elias Whaley was the yardman and foreman at the Grimball Plantation during the farming season. People called him by his nickname [Papa Light]. Elias was captain of the Seminole boat that was use to haul vegetable from the Grimball's, Dill's, McLeod and the Seabrook's docks down the Stono Rivers, Wappoo Cut and Ashley Rivers to Adgers Wharf on the Cooper Rivers to Charleston.

The property where Bucks Lumber Company is located on Maybank Highway was all farmlands. The Dills use to lease it to the Nungezer Farms. George Nungezer had the contract to supply Campbell Soup Company with green beans, tomatoes and many other vegetables. He later leased the property in the Whitehouse section of Fort Johnson on the island; then moved his farming operations there. That when your daddy went to work for him in 1920. Man, I tell you that German, Nungezer was a mean white man.

One summer day in 1923, after the overseer, Fuller King, paid my grandpa for his vegetables, minus the rent; Grandpa told him that was not enough money. King told my grandpa if he didn't like the amount he was paid, he could take his family and get the hell off the damn plantation! After he left, my grandpa held his hand to his face; I think he wept.

He was behind the house and did not realize I was there. It would be the only time I saw him seem to be crying; he was a physically and mentally strong man. Grandma Miley told me later the Buckra King paid Grandpa just enough money to buy food that week. Following slavery until the late 1940s, the black men and women answer white folks "yes sur boss," and, "yes ma'am" but behind their back called them Buckra and Cracker.

I had many conversations with my grandpa, your grandpa and many slaves from other plantations about slavery over the years. Son if you could have herded those men tells how the white men on the plantations treated them it makes you want to cry and then get a gun and do some killing. Grandpa said during slavery, the Massa gave them one pair of high top shoes a year during Christmas time. If the shoe did not last the year, they had to tie rags with string and wire around it to make it last or walked bare feet.

He said the white men had baby with their wives and daughters and the husband could say or do nothing. Look at all of the half-white people on this island. You don't have to look far—look at me, look in the Chisolm, Lawton, Gilliard, Matthew, Mack, White, Blake, Brown and the Wallace; all have mulatto in they family. Our ancestor did not come from Africa look like this. Before integration, if a black man stares at white women, the white man was ready to lynch him.

Grandpa and the majority of slaves and sharecropper I talk with said the Seabrooks and Legares were plantations owners that sell or gave property to a few of the slaves. The slaves that were given property by the Freedmen's Bureau from McLeod Plantation was taken from them and give back to the plantation owners. The Grimballs and the Clarks sold property to the slaves at a rate they could afford during and following slavery. The other plantations owners gave slaves nothing.

Following slavery, the Dills sold property to a few slaves. They refuse to give property to the slaves that made them wealthy by the sweat of brows working on the plantation all they lives. Your grandpa was their private chauffeur all his life and they gave him nothing, not even enough land to build a house. Instead the property that was not sold to whites, the Dill sisters in a "Will" left the 1,264 acres of the plantation to the Charleston Museum to manage as a wildlife refuge.

In 1988, the nonprofit organizations sold the land to developers and divide the money among the charitable organizations, after the Dill sisters' will was broken, influenced by the City Administration. None benefit the black people that help made the Dills rich on James Island, except the 280 acres condemn for the Charleston County Park on Riverland Drive which all citizen is allowed to use.

When I was a young boy, your mother, Sis uses to walks your uncle Scoot [James Smalls] and me to Cut Bridge School. The school was at the bridge near the entrance where Charleston County Park is built on Riverland Drive. It was two mile from our cabin. The school building was in the marsh next to the small creek and when the tide was high, water would flood the schoolyards and the students would get wet.

After we get out of school, Sis would come back and take us to the cotton field. This cotton field was about one hundred acre. This was the early 1900s. The field was located in the area where the Carolina Skyway Airport was later build next to King Solomon Lodge Hall, on Stono Road [Riverland Drive].

Your mother would walk's us to the cotton field to your grandma Lucy; she would tie a croakers bag around our waist. The bag would be long enough to touch the ground and hold at least ten pound of cotton. The overseers pay the people one cent per pound for the first picking and two cents for the second. It took a long time to pick a pound of them damn cotton. Some time the field would be boggy from the rain, but if the cotton was dry the people still had to pick them.

Sometime the foreman would have the cottons taken to the Dills' storage shed by mules and wagons. If the field was too wet for the mule to pull the wagon, the peoples had to carry the bundle of cotton on top of their head, and walked the two mile from the field to the shed. The overseer would weigh the cottons and then tell the people to come back on Friday to be paid their one cent a pound.

There is a slave cemetery at the end of that field near the Stono River, called Devil Nest, next to the Grimballs Plantation. A lot of slaves buried there from Turkey Pen area. There is another slave cemetery on Riverland Drive not far from the Dill house. That is where your grandpa Dan, his wife, your sister, brother, my mother, stepfather, grandpa, grandma and the rest of the slaves from Turkey Pen are all buried.

Whenever the slaves/sharecropper wants to have a secret meeting that night, while working in the fields during the day, they would sing that song, "I am going to lay down my burden down by the riverside." In the song, would be the location where the meeting would be held. The overseer never knew the song was use as a signal by the people. On many occasions, the overseer wanted to hear the people sing the song over, and over again. Afterward, the people would laugh about how they made a fool of the overseer.

The Dills had a commissary store on Fort Johnson Road, across the road from where the black St. James Presbyterian Church is today. The Dills at one time paid the people on the farm with they own paper money that you had to spend at the store. I remember a lot of time my mama would send me to the store for corn flour, and molasses.

On several occasions I would buy Johnnycake, root beer, Pepsi and Royal Crown drinks. Each cost three cents; during those days black people could not buy Coke. One day in 1924, while I was in the store, a black man asks for a Coke, I think he was a World War I veteran; he was wearing an army uniform, the white man said, "nigger, you know you all not allow to buy Coke, you better buy this big nigger's drinks or get the hell out of here!"

The black man walks out the store with his head bow down. When I went outside, he sent me back inside, to buy him a Royal Crown drink and a Johnnycake. I never forgot the sad look on his face and wonder why he said nothing, but Grandpa told me it was best that he say nothing if he didn't want trouble. The Dills sold everything in the store, clothes, military surplus material, flour, butts meat, pork, fatback, molasses and lard. I learned later James Brooks Williams was the soldier the white man called a nigger. Harry Haley would later operate the store.

If it were not for the black men fishing with their cast net and picking oyster, sharing their catch with the community, I don't know how some of the black people would survive during the sharecrop/farming time on the Dill Plantation. They were paying our peoples just enough money to buy foods and seeds minus rent.

I am going to tell you something funny, it was not funny when it happened, but it shore as hell seem funny now. My uncle Elias Urie was a smart young man and did not believe in hard work. Said he was not going to work on any white man plantation for one dollar and fifty cent per week. His nickname was "Pick." One night he was trying to steal a wagon wheel from Thomas Middleton shed, who incidentally was one of the black constables for James Island.

Middleton heard the noise and came outside with his shotgun, he fire at the man running in the dark, hitting Uncle Pick in the arm. The next day Uncle Elias and his wife Celia pack their suitcases and left town for New Jersey in 1944. He never came back home; he died in New Jersey sometime during the late 1950s. Aunt Celia visits your mother, Sis, regular during the summer's month until she died some time during the 1960s.

Thomas Middleton Jr. and my mother confirmed Harry's recollection of this incident. In 1956, while in the United States Army, I drove my mother on a short vacation trip to visit Aunt Celia in New Jersey; during the visit they joked about the incident.

I know you heard about this but I'm going to tell you anyway. My grandpa Hump said during the Civil War, the slave master would have one of his slaves dig a hole and bury his money in an iron chest, fearing that the Yankee would overrun them and find their money. I suspect they were some black people here on James Island that could have found money. Grandpa said this old man use to rent the property called Birch from the Dills to farms. The property is where the James Island Senior Citizens Center is now on Riverland Drive, not far from the Stono River.

While he was plowing the fields, one of his sons saw the end of a chain sticking out of the ground. They pull up the chains and found that it was connected to an iron chest, dug it up and discover money inside. During the 1800s, they was able to buy all those property, build a two-story house for their family and then buy land for a private cemetery at Central Park and Fleming Road, you tell me where the money came from?

I was draft in the U.S. Army in 1942, when I return home from World War II in 1944, Edward "Neddie" Grimball sent for me. He gave me $5,500 to get started in life. He told me because of the time, white people did not accept blacks in the white race especially in the South. Neddie said my mother was a good woman, but that was the way thing had to be during the time. He sent for me the second time but he died before I went back to see him in 1960. I bought this property and built this house with the money he gave me.

I was aware of Harry being the son of a white man, even if one did not know his father. There was no doubt looking at him; besides, my mother had told me years before that Harry's father was a white man from Johns Island. Census records show an Eddie L. "Neddie" Grimball (1882–1960) of Johns Island; Harry said he was his father.

Harry continued,

I know you familiar with J. Arthur Brown, when you were a member of the NAACP back in the early 1960s, he was the president; before you joined the police department. Arthur told me that his father was William Hinson, the plantation owner in Fort Johnson. That's how he got his start in life. His mother did domestic work for Hinson.

By 1944, most of the black and white people knew about me and other half-white on the island. You can look at the census report and see how many people listed as mulatto for race. The white plantations owner and overseer father had babies with just about every black family on the island—beginning with me. All have mulatto in their family. Take a look at the research you doing, after the slaves were set free following the signing of the Emancipation Proclamation; most all of the mulatto people on the island end up with property and money that the white men provide for them.

Very few dark skin blacks were well off during that same period except the ones that were freedmen during slavery. This was some of the tactic use by the white men to continue keeping the black race divide, instilled in them that light skin black was superior to dark black, and the white men were superior to everyone. I know you familiar with Liza Matthews; she lives next door to your family. Raymond Grimball fathered a child with her.

The child was sent up North to live; the affair was no secret. Most people on the island knew about it. Raymond use to be at her house all time of day and night. The property next to Little Rock Golf Club was own by Raymond Grimball. He deeded the property to Liza and had a house built for her.

During the early 1940s, Willamae and her children came back home to live with her mother Liza. She enrolled them in school but later she would move back to the North. Raymond offered to sell your daddy the property next to the Frazier's. When your daddy could not come up with the money, Raymond sold it to Richard Smalls, my uncle, where he build the Little Rock Golf Club.

Harry Urie was a proud man; he was considered a historian on James Island. He will be remembered as such. Harry died on December 27, 2002, shortly after I had my last interview with him. I enjoyed talking with him over the years about the history of James Island. I know of no person on the island who possessed the knowledge that Harry did concerning its history.

I remember Harry's mother and stepfather, Joseph Gadsden; people called him by his nickname, "Jill." Many times when my mother and I visited Turkey Pen, Jill would be drinking his whiskey from a half-pint bottle. My mother called his wife Cousin Nennie; she would sometimes argue with him about his drinking. I remember her being a sweet, congenial person. Many times my mother and I walked by her house during the hot summer months. She would chip pieces of ice from her icebox beside the house and give us a cold drink of water.

Hump Urie Jr. (1899–1971) and his wife Etta (Child) Smalls (1900–1999) had three sons, Daniel, Harry and Alonzo; and four daughters, Inez, Evelyn, Sarah and Miley.

Etta Urie was the oldest surviving child of my grandpa's children. She and her husband Hump were farmers on the Dill Plantation. My mother called Aunt Etta "Child" and Hump "Budall." I recalled Uncle Budall doing some farming, but he worked at a fertilizer plant in Charleston. The latter part of his life he worked in a

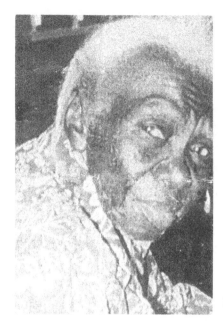

Etta Eurie. *Family photograph.*

lumber mill until he became disabled. The entire area where Queensboro is located at the end of Turkey Pen was a lumber mill during the 1930s throughout the 1940s.

During the farming season, I recalled their sons, Harry, Dan and Alonzo, doing most of the plowing and cultivating the farms. When it was time to harvest the vegetables, all her children would help with the chores. The vegetables would be placed in boxes, bushel baskets and crates and taken to Charleston market on Meeting Street by Aunt Child to be sold.

Tuesdays, Thursdays and Saturdays were the days the black farmers took their vegetables to the Charleston market. Aunt Child would catch rides with James Bennett (Son Bennett)—one of the few blacks who was fortunate enough to own a truck from the late 1930s through the late 1940s. Hump Urie and his son Alonzo are buried in the Dill slave cemetery. Etta Urie is buried in Payne Church's cemetery.

Grandpa lived with Aunt Child from 1950 until he died in 1954. However, he did live with my parents on the Grimball Plantation on two separate occasions, but he never got used to living any place besides the wilderness. That was where he had become accustomed to browsing around in the woods.

Cesar Smalls (1861–1958) and his wife Charity (1871) had one son, Daniel (1908). Cesar was the carpenter for the plantation. He built and repaired cabins for the people. He also built coffins for the dead on the plantation during the era of slavery and sharecropping.

Joseph Bennett (1870) and his wife Martha Bennett (1860) had a grandson, Elijah (1898); and two stepsons, William Brown (1882) and Samuel Brown (1886). Also living in the household were Julia McFall (1893) and Isabel Carr (1899), both schoolteachers and both mulattos.

James Bennett (1876) and his wife Lizzie (1879) had one daughter, Susan (1892); and two sons, James Jr. (1901) and Christopher (1899).

I remember James Bennett Jr. (1901). He lived near the battery not far from the Goss's. He owned one of those small model Ford pickup trucks that the farmer's wife depends on for transportation to the market. People that lived on the plantation called him "Son Bennett." He would drive the women and their vegetables to the market in downtown Charleston from the Turkey Pen area during the farming and sharecropping era.

Aunt Etta Urie was one of his regular riders on Tuesday, Thursday and Saturday. Son Bennett would drive my Aunt Etta from the Dill Plantation in Turkey Pen to our house on the Grimball Plantation on several occasions during the weekend. Son Bennett was a short man, about five foot two. One of his legs was shorter than the other and I remember times when he became arrogant as hell for the least thing. However, this incident was different.

I recall one Sunday evening in 1943; he brought my Aunt Etta to our house to see my mother. While he was there talking with my father he said,

> *Boise, I wok on dat farm plowin mule un clearin land for twenty yea for King un Park. I am not gonna wok another goddamn day for them! I waz plowin the oter day, un dat mule kick the shits out of me. I took my whip un cut his ass. You know dat goddamn Park Mikell tells me if I hit his mule again he would do the same ting to me.*
>
> *Boise, I ask dat s.o.b. if he tink his goddamn mule waz better un colored people? Park told me to take my family, un get the hell off his plantation; dat is exactly what I do. This piece of truck I got I am gonna haul people to the market, un make a livin the best way I can. I ain't gonna to wok like a goddamn slave the rest of my life to help make them goddamn cracker get rich un me un my family lives in misery.*

I was young, but I knew it took a lot of courage to stand up to a white man and say the things he said during those turbulent years, taking the stand that he did not knowing where he and his family would go or live.

Frank Gadsden (1830–1885) and his wife Peggy (1831–1895) had one son, Frank (1855); and three daughters, Ann (1848), Abigail (1858) and Lydia (1859).

Peggy Gadsden and her daughter Lydia were injured during the 1893 storm, when her house was picked up off its foundation and thrown to another part of the Dill Plantation. This information was corroborated and substantiated by several people, including Hettie Gadsden Prioleau (1872), who was the niece of Peggy, Mary Chavis Frazier (1880) and Frank Deleston (1875).

Joseph Gadsden (1838) and his wife Charlotte Johnson Gadsden (1840) had five daughters, Betsy (1856), Hanna (1868), Hettie (1872), Alice (1875) and Janie (1876); and one son, Robert (1866).

Hettie Gadsden Prioleau (1872–1986) and her husband Walter Prioleau Sr. (1871–1949) had two sons, Harry (1914) and Walter Jr., (1923–2004); and four daughters, Elouise (1911), Lucile (1916–1956), Victoria (1920) and Edith (1929).

Hettie Prioleau (1874–1986). *Family photograph.*

Conversations with Hettie Gadsden Prioleau

Hettie, the third oldest daughter of Joseph and Charlotte Gadsden, told me,

> *I waz born and raised on Dill Plantation. My Pa un Ma waz slaves. From time I waz six yea old my bubber, four sisters un me had to get up fore da sunrise in da mornin, wen it waz still dark, rooster crow, un da otersear ring da big bell. All da people live on da plantation had to wok from sunrise to sundown. I tell yu. Man we had it hard. We plant da seed in da ground duin plantin time. Wen weeds grow round the plants, we pull it wid our hand even in rains.*
>
> *Dey house we live in waz in front of da tall Battery wid a lot of oter houses; we house waz parted into three rooms, wid cardboard, two board window, un a door dat swing outside. We had no stove, Pa un Ma use chimney to heat da house un cook food. In wintertime, I tell yu it waz hard; we did not have no warm clothe; but we pray to God all da time for a better life.*
>
> *Wen it rains we wid put bucket on da floor under leak to catch rainwater wen it pour to da roof. My bubber Robert left home wen he waz a young boy; we never saw him gain. Pa and Ma tried to find him, but never did, somebody tell Pa dat a white man took him to Savannah, Georgia, but dat all we know. Them white man on da plantation waz mean to my Pa. Wen dey get mad, dey wid cuss Pa! He wid plow fields wid mule, un drive wagon to haul cuttin, tater un corn. Them Dills pay people on da plantation one cent a pound to pick cotton.*
>
> *Yu no wen dem wagon un mule bogs in da mud, dey otersear make we push them out. Wen time to geter corn un tater da otersear come to we house at night suchin to see if my Pa teaf [steal] any corn or tater, wen them white man get mad dey call my Pa and oter black peoples nigger. Lota yea we did not have shoes to wear; we walk round in summer on farms*

barefoot. We had one pair of upper shoes to wear un we mostly put it on in da wintertime. Duin winter month, everyone wid geter in front of da chimney to keep warm at night.

We live next to Aunt Peggy duin da 1893 stom. Ms. Peggy waz married tu my uncle, Frank Gadsden [1830]. He dead fore dey 1893 stom. Cousin Peggy house waz pick up by da stom and chunk down in a oter place. Cousin Peggy un one of hur chillin waz in da house un got hut bad. I tink Peggy dead from da hut [injuries] she got from da storm bout six mont after dat. It waz hard time duin them days to get a doctor to tend yu; a lota oter people got hut doing da storm.

I waz glad wen Walter start comin tu see me. He lives on da Grimball Plantation wid his family. Dey own da land wha he lives. I got married tu Walter un moved tu dey farm wha we raised our chillin. Reason I walks round barefoot, it a habit from da old time wen Pa could not ford to buy we shoes.

We had to wok on them farm barefoot un save our one shoe for winter mont wen it was cold. Many time over da yea I wid go wid Feedie [Mary Roper] to liver babies on da island. I like tu help brin chillin in the wold. The reason we made it through them hard time cause we pray un believe in God.

Hettie Prioleau was a very religious and congenial woman who always had a kind word for everyone and always greeted you with a smile. I met Hettie's granddaughter, Francis Prioleau, in 1958 while in the U.S. Army stationed at Fort Jackson, South Carolina. We got married in 1959. After marrying her granddaughter, Hettie and I would have numerous conversations over the next 27 years concerning those turbulent years in her family life growing up on the farm and the enslavement of her parents. She was a lifelong member of the St. James Presbyterian Church on James Island. Hettie would live a long and prosperous life until her death in 1986, at the age of 114; she was buried in the Burn Church Cemetery at the corner of Folly and Fort Johnson Road.

Over thirty years ago, unknown to me, my daughter Geraldine, as a teenager, had a conversation with her great-grandmother Hettie concerning her life and the loss of her brother Robert. She never forgot the light in Hettie's eyes when, as a child, with only the assurance that a child can give, Geraldine proclaimed that she would one day find Robert. The story of Robert never was forgotten by my daughter who, though involved in her own life as teenagers are, as a young adult still carried the memories of that conversation with her great-grandmother and never completely gave up hope of finding Robert. She thought at one point, some twenty years later, that she had a lead when planning the first ever Gadsden reunion. However, the link between Robert and the family in question could not be established. It is our hope that if this book does not find some information on the whereabouts of Robert that at least his story will serve as our dedication to Hettie on the love and the hope that she always maintained on being with her brother. If she could dictate these last words, I am sure that she would write, "Son, you can rest assured for I have at last been reunited with my brother, Robert."

According to statements made by my grandmother, Mary Chavis Frazier, and Frank Deleston, they corroborate and substantiate Hettie's statement concerning the 1893

Alfred Smalls, photo taken by a pilot from Carolina Sky Way Airport. *Family photograph.*

storm. They said Peggy never fully recovered from the injury before she died. Their account of this incident was also substantiated by information obtained from the archives.

Isaac Gadsden (1867) and his wife Celia (1871) had five sons, John (1899), Ben (1904), Robert (1905), William (1907) and Richard (1908); and three daughters, Mary (1910), Ann (1913) and Liza (1918).

Isaac Smalls (1874) and his wife Margaret (1884) had four sons, John (1916), Elijah (1922), Thomas (1927) and Harrison (1928); and two daughters, Louise (1908) and Lucile (1926), all listed as mulatto.

Alfred Smalls (1894) and his wife Rosa Gladden Smalls had four sons, Alfred Jr., John, Franklin and Ernest; and two daughters, Wilhelmina and Ernestine.

An unknown pilot flying over Turkey Pen from the Carolina Sky Way Airport on Riverland Drive took the above picture. It shows Alfred pushing a planter's plow, sometimes called a horseless plow, planting seeds on his farm. The photo was taken during the late 1930s or early 1940s; the picture was furnished by Evelyn Urie, daughter of Etta and Hump Urie, of Turkey Pen.

James W. Scott (1915) and his wife Mary Leize (1916) had six daughters, Shirley, Joyce, Vermell, Sheila, Dorothy and Bell. I sat in Mr. Scott's front room in his house located on Riverland Drive on July 12, 2005, talking with him and his daughter, Dorothy. I knew Mr. Scott from my youth and throughout adulthood in the community and affectionately called him by his nickname, "Blungie." He stood approximately six feet tall and was of slender build. I found him to be an honest and congenial person whom everyone in the community loved.

Frazier, when I was a young boy, me, my brothers and sisters all worked on the farms; my brother Israel did not like the farm life so he moved to the City of Charleston when he was young. I started working on the Dill farm when "Old Man King" was running the farm. I plowed with mules, digs potatoes, break corns, pick beans and cotton. I work with men like Franklin Gilliard. He was married to my sister Bertha. Isaac Kinlock and a lot of other men—we were paid ten cent a day during those years.

Your grandpa, Dan Smalls, was the Dills' and Kings' private chauffeur during the time, driving them around in a horse and buggy around the plantation, and driving the Dills' daughters to school. Old man Charlie Goss was made a foreman after slavery during sharecrop and farming time. One of Charlie's hand and arm was cut at his elbow by Dill cotton machine. The people use to call him "Yubber" and "Cowboy Charlie," as he rides his horse around the farm. Jeffery Lemon was brought in by Park Mikell when he took over the farm and was made foreman.

We did not have electric light doing the 1920s through the 1940s. Our parents use a kerosene oil lamp with a glass shade to see at night. We use well water that was pump out of the ground by a hand pump, and a three-foot tin tub to take our bath in at night. In the winter months, we would heat the water in the chimney fireplace at night. They were tough times working on the farm, from sunrise to sundown. We work hard. We were paid ten cent a day. If you were late getting to work, Mr. King would cut that same dime to five cent. I work on the Dill farm until I got married.

I got a job working at the Charleston Naval Shipyard in 1944. I was lucky during the time it was the best job a black man could hope to get in Charleston and earn a decent wage to support his family. I retire in 1980 from the shipyard after working for thirty-seven years.

All that property where the Municipal Golf Course is now, in the Cut Bridges section, from Maybank Highway all the way back to Riverland Drive, to the Stono River, was own by the Dills. After slavery, the Dills refuse to give the slaves any of the property and sell most to a white man name Myers. He was running a farm in the Riverland Terrace area.

Before Myers left Charleston, he sold most of the property in Fergerson Village to black people for price they could afford, including the property where I live on today. He also sold property to the Washingtons and many others in Fergerson Village. You know J. Arthur Brown. He usta live down there on Camp Road, until he die. J. Arthur look like a white man.

His mother used to do domestic work for old man William Hinson, he was the owner of the Hinson Plantation in Fort Johnson section. We was talking one day about the white man having baby with our black women. Arthur told Harry Urie and me that Hinson was his daddy, and gave him his start in life. Harry's daddy was also a white man. Frazier, our peoples made it this far through those hard time praying to God and hard work; we should always pray and give God the praise and the glory, amen.

Peter Nowell Sr. (1894) and his wife Molsie (1895-1974) had two sons, Peter Jr. (1912) and Daniel (1918–1995); and five daughters, Julia (1916), Anna Bell (1917), Mattie (1925), Earline (1925) and Mary Leise (1927). Molsie also raised a granddaughter, Lillie Mae Nowell (1928).

Peter Sr. and Peter Jr. are buried in the Dill Slave Cemetery on Riverland Drive. After the death of her husband, Peter Sr., Molsie moved her family from Turkey Pen to Riverland Drive, next to the Johnson and Gethers families, during the late 1930s.

Peter Nowell Jr. (1910–1946) and his wife Mary Sanders (1913) had one son, Buster; and one daughter, Evelyna "Mag" Sanders. Peter and his family lived in Turkey Pen until his death in 1946. He and my father were friends. I recall going to the Nowell house on Turkey Pen with my father to visit on many occasions. Peter was known by his nickname, Len.

Daniel Nowell Sr. (1918–1995) and his wife Earnestine had eight sons, Daniel Jr., Nathaniel, Remus, Ernest, Bernard, Larry, Freddie T. and Robert B.; and five daughters, Annabell, Rosalee H., Lillie Mae, Carolyn and Lottie Mae.

Arthur Brown (1909) and his wife Mae De had one son, Greg; and three daughters, Minerva, Joenelle and Millicent E. Mr. Brown was a prominent businessman in the Charleston area involved in the real estate business. He was a civic leader in the community for decades and was president of the local chapter of the NAACP for several years before and during the integration crisis.

He was credited with filing the first lawsuit in Charleston on behalf of his daughter, Micellent E. Brown, charging the Charleston County School Board with racial discrimination in reference to the education of black students. This lawsuit would be combined with others out of Topeka, Kansas, to become the landmark decision *Brown vs. the Board of Education.*

Clarence Fergerson (1862) was married to Julia Fergerson Brown (1865). They had three sons, Stephen (1878), Arthur (1884) and Gillie Brown (1882); and two daughters, Ella (1880) and Rose (1885). Clarence and Julia are listed among the founding fathers and mothers of Payne Church.

Stephen Brown (1878) and his wife Amelia (1880) had three sons, Rodger (1914), Murphy (1916) and Sidney (1917); one daughter, Thomacena (1920); two granddaughters, Agnes Smalls (1919) and Wilimenia Brown (1926); and two grandsons, Junius Brown (1928) and Thomas Kershaw (1919).

Cyrus Pinckney Sr. (1871) and his wife Catherine (1872) had two sons, Cyrus Jr. (1906) and Joseph (1898); and three daughters, Rena (1895), Henrietta (1898) and Eleanor (1909); all were mulattos. Also living with them were a son in-law, George Holmes (1886); one granddaughter, Catherine (1912); and grandson Herman Holmes.

Cyrus Pinckney (1906) and his wife Eleanor had seven sons, Leroy, Alonzo, Harold, Irvin, Christopher, Earl and Cyrus Jr.; and three daughters, Melvina, Emily and Rena.

James Brisbane (1862) and his wife Mariah (1864) had six daughters, Roxanna (1890), Susan (1892), Henrietta (1894), Estelle (1899), Viola (1901) and Wilimenia (1903); and one son, Swackie (1905).

The Bethel AME Church was organized in 1868 under the leadership of Reverend Lucas, in that section of James Island known as Cross Cut, located at the corners of Central Park Road and Fleming Road. According to the church's history, it struggled under the leadership of several pastors. In 1968, the original structure was rebuilt under the leadership of Reverend Frank Smalls (1897), assisted by Reverend James Brisbane (1891) and Reverend Coleman Forrest (1895).

Pastors included Reverend Elijah Green from 1971 to 1978, Reverend Leon Townsend from 1978 to 1983, Reverend Jeremiah McKinley from 1983 to 1987 and the Reverend Luther J. Gibbs from 1987 to the present. Some of the older members of the church, listed as the church's mothers, included Hattie Scott, Alma Singelton, Louise Hezekiah and David Hezekiah. In 2005, a new church was completed by members on Central Park Road under the leadership of Reverend Gibbs.

Amos Riley (1892) and his wife Edith (1900) had one son, Harrison (1917); and five daughters, Hester (1918), Patsy (1922), Celia (1925), Martha (1928) and Lou (1929).

John Black (1850) and his wife Mary (1855) had one daughter, Julia Black Forest (1883); and a grandson, Benjamin Black (1892). All were mulattos. Also living with the family was nephew James Brisbane (1894).

Noah Black (1860) was a widower. He had one son, Holling Black (1890); both were mulattos. Noah Black, according to history, was one of the slaves given forty

Bernice Black Stewart. *Family photograph.*

acres following the end of slavery. Holling Black (1890) and his wife Bessie Hamilton (1896) had one daughter, Bernice (1916). Mr. Black was a farmer and a carpenter.

Bernice Black Stewart (1916) and her husband Daniel Stewart (1914–1958) had two sons, Alfred (1934–1968) and Daniel Jr. (1936–1978); and three daughters, Ruthel (1937), Loretta (1939) and Elizabeth (1941).

I interviewed Mrs. Stewart in her front room along with her niece, Connie, on one hot day in June 2004. Although Ms. Stewart had problems with her eyes, she seemed at ease with herself. She said, "Now tell me, who you is?" I responded, "My daddy was Sandy Frazier. People in the community called him 'Boise.' My mother was Viola Frazier. They called her 'Sis.' She was the daughter of Lucy and Daniel Smalls."

She continued,

Son, I know all of your family. Your mama and my mama were cousins. I know your sister, Julia Frazier. She is close to this family; but first let me tell you about me. My daddy name was Holling Black and my mother name was Bessie Hamilton Black. I was the only child in the family. I had a brother but he died real young.

My daddy was one of the biggest black farmers on James Island. When I was a young girl, he own land all over Cut Bridge, on Fleming Road and Holling Road. I was blessed; I did not have to work on the farms like the rest of the children. Besides being a farmer, my daddy was a carpenter. He works for Colburg Dairy and help build many of the building for the company.

I went to Cut Bridge School. The building was in the marsh of Stono Road by the little bridge. Our teacher's name was Ms. Murry and Ms. Wainwright. The school only went to the eighth grade. They were no high school on James Island for black people. When I was young, we didn't join the church like the people do today. We had to go out in the wilderness, seek and pray. That mean it could be in the woods, behind a barn or an empty building away from the house. During the many weeks that we prayed, we would tell our dreams to leaders in meetings at Jerusalem Lodge Hall on Riverland Drive. After several weeks of praying, you would be told who your leader was, and what church you belong to. Children of today don't have the faith we had in those days.

I remember one night in 1931 or 1932, several of us young girl was going to a meeting at Jerusalem Lodge Hall on Riverland Drive; when we got there people was crying on the porch that Ms. Betsy Gladden had die inside while the meeting was going on. I think she had a heart attack.

I meet my husband Dan one evening when I went to a meeting with my parents at King Solomon Lodge Hall. I saw this tall handsome boy standing behind me in the lodge hall while the people was praying, singing and shouting.

After the meeting, Martha Richardson, my girlfriend, and me walk out ahead of our parents. He walked up behind us in the yard while I was waiting on my parent. He asks me my name. "Why you want to know my name?" "I been watching you a long time, I like you, and want to be your boyfriend." "I don't know you." "But, I know you." That how we met and start talking.

Dan and I got married in 1934; we had those five beautiful children I mention earlier. I love all of them dearly, but you know; they is always one that is your pet and mine was Daniel Jr. I used to cuddle and hug him. After he became a big boy, he would come home from school or from socializing and would tell me all the news. My son, Alfred, would tell him, "Boy, shut your mouth. You talks too much." I got a laugh out of that.

Dan worked on Folly Beach Pier for a while, but he got a job working at the Charleston Naval Shipyard in 1939. He worked there until he took sick and was taken to the hospital where he died in 1958. Son, I had several opportunities to get married again, but I had a good life with my husband and children. I just was not interested again. The people on James Island made it through those hard times because of their belief in God and prayer, that is what the world need today.

I found Ms. Stewart to be a congenial, articulate and friendly person to talk with. I remember my mother always talked about her cousin, Bessie Hamilton Black, who was the mother of Ms. Stewart. During my high school years at Burke, I have to admit having a secret crush on her daughter Ruthel; of course, I don't believe Ruthel ever knew about my teenage crush on her before I joined the United States Army.

William Stewart (1876) and his wife Julia (1885) had one son, Daniel (1915), as well as a mother-in-law, Ellen Grant (1835), who lived with them.

Paul (Commodore) Hamilton (1863) and his wife Mariah (1863) had two sons, Chris (1895) and Benjamin (1900); and two daughters, Jolene (1885) and Bessie (1896).

Benjamin Hamilton (1903) and his wife Ruth (1911–2003) had four sons, Benjamin, Melvin, Leroy, Isaac; a stepson, James; and six daughters, Naomi, Edith, Mary, Livinia, Rebecca and Francis.

I recall between the ages of seven and ten that on many occasions I would accompany my mother and sisters on the Dill farm. I recall my mother telling us that Mr. Ben and Mrs. Ruth were her cousins.

Scipio Hamilton (1865) and his wife Rina (1868) had two daughters, Emily (1910) and Florence (1912); one grandson, Isaac Wilder (1912); two granddaughters, Anna (1915) and Hattie Johnson (1912); and grandchildren Willie Johnson (1925), Lillian Chisolm (1927) and Walter (1915).

Alex Hamilton (1884) and his wife Victoria (1904) had three daughters, Mary Leise (1914), Evelina (1917) and Janie (1922); and three sons, Peter (1918), Alex Jr. (1924) and James (1928).

Jonas Smalls (1877) and his wife Rose Richardson (1878) had three sons, Alfred (1894), Frank (1897) and Henry (1907). After the death of his first wife Rose, Jonas married Adele Simmons Smalls (1892); they had one daughter, Victoria (1922).

Levy Gilliard (1843) and his wife Susan (1845) had one son, Levy (1884). Levy had a son, Franklin (1904), with Mary Deleston prior to his marriage to Susan Gilliard, according to information furnished by Franklin Gilliard's daughter, Albertha Jenkins.

Franklin Gilliard (1904) and his wife Bertha (1906) had four sons, Franklin Jr., James (Bosie), Levy and Harold; and five daughters, Elouise, Julie, Martha, Helen and Albertha. Also living with the family was a brother of Bertha, William Scott, according to the 1920 census report.

Albertha Gilliard Jenkins, the daughter of Franklin, said,

> *During Daddy's young age, he worked on the Dill farm for many years. His second job was working with a construction company paving Folly Road during 1929 through the 1930s, until it was completed. He then got a job working at the Charleston Naval Shipyard where he worked for eighteen years. After he left the Charleston Naval Shipyard, he worked for the Jewish synagogue for twenty-two years before he retired.*
>
> *He bought the property on Riverland Drive in the front of Fergerson Village where we were raised. When it became known that the people living in Fergerson Village did not have access to their property from Riverland Drive, Daddy donated some of his property so the people could have a "right of way" to their home and property. That was the kind of person daddy was. He was a member of First Baptist Church on Camp Road and chairmen of the Deacon Board for many years.*

Cornelius Richardson Sr. (1896) and his wife Margaret (1900) had six sons, Benjamin (1915–1971), Dennis (1918), Limus (1920), William (1921), Cornelius Jr. (1926) and Earl (1929); and one daughter, Ethel (1924).

William Richardson, the fourth child of Cornelius and Margaret Richardson, was born and raised on James Island. William and his brothers grew up on the farms. William said,

> *Frazier, my family farmed ten acres of land on both sides of Camp Road. My brothers and I worked on the farm planting and harvesting the vegetables for our parents to sell on the market to support us during those hard years.*
>
> *I went to Cut Bridge Elementary School, just across the road from our house on Camp Road and Riverland Drive. After I finished elementary school, there were no high schools on James Island for blacks during the 1920s, '30s and 1940s. Those of us who wanted a high school education had to attend Burke High School in the City of Charleston.*
>
> *As you know there were no public transportation from James Island to Charleston and the State of South Carolina refused to furnish school buses for "colored," that what white people called blacks during that era. So we had to walk the five miles to school. Sometime we were lucky enough to catch rides with the few blacks that owned cars on the island. I was drafted into the United States Army in World War II.*

Thomas Walton Jr. (1923–2004) and his wife Josephine D. (1928) had two daughters, Vernal Walton and Audrey Harley. On a number of occasions, I visited Thomas at his residence while he sat in his lazy boy chair in his front room. In my talks with him, it was obvious that he was a proud black man. He said to me,

> *Frazier let me tell you, I was raised just like many of the young boys growing up on James Island. Our parents strongly believed in God and prayer.*

When I was a young boy growing up, my brothers and I had lot of chores to do. I went to Cut Bridge School about a mile from here on Riverland Drive. The school was sitting in the marsh by the small bridge and at one time the road was called Stono Road. After I finished elementary school, there were no high schools on James Island for black people. The people that wanted a high school education had to attend Burke Industrial High School in the City of Charleston. Frazier, during my time growing up, it was not easy getting to school in the City from James Island.

I worked for Youngblood Construction Company for a while. If you wanted to make life better for your family, it takes faith, hard work and determination. I got a job at the Charleston Naval Base Shipyard and worked there for thirty-seven years before I retired. In 1947, I married my wife Josephine.

Thomas's love for his wife was obvious as he talked on one occasion to Edward McKelvey and me when we visited him during the time he was sick. As he talked and we sat and listened, he said, "I married the most beautiful woman on James Island." As he smiled, he said, "I don't know why these men want to play with women in the street if they love what is at home."

Thomas was a member of the St. James Presbyterian Church, and he held virtually every officer position in the church. He was one of the original founders of the Sons of Elijah Masonic Lodge #457 on James Island and was elected its second worshipful master. He was also one of its worthy patrons as well as the Daughters of Elijah Eastern Star #337. Thomas died in 2004, shortly after my last visit with him. He was considered one of the pillars in the community.

Alonzo Moore (1924) and his wife Isadora D. (1926) had four sons, Alonzo, Lawrence, Hazel Reese and Ronnie J.; and eight daughters, Emily, Ida, Evelyn, Hazel, Lorraine, Dolly Ann, Lida and Yvonne.

Alonzo was known in the Cut Bridge Community by his nickname, "Lonzo." He worked on the Dill Plantation when Park Mikell was the manager. As a young boy beginning at the age of seven, I used to accompany my mother and sisters on the farm picking green beans and bagging Irish potatoes. Lonzo was one of the men who drove the farm tractors and trucks, plowed the fields and took the beans and potatoes to railroad stations to be shipped to other states.

I remembered Lonzo as being a humble, quiet and gentle man. He had a unique pleasant look on his face when he smiled. I recall while working on the farm that my mother would point to certain people and say they were our cousins. During one of these incidents, she pointed to Lonzo and his wife Isadora and told me that my grandfather, Sandy Frazier Sr., and Isadora's father, Joe Deleston, were first cousins. While he worked on the farm, Lonzo would always stop and talk with my mother.

John Sanders (1872) and his wife Margaret Brown (1882) had two daughters, Mary (1903) and Mary Leise (1913); and two sons, Abraham (1916) and Benjamin (1923). Mary would marry Isaac Kinlock, and Mary Leise would marry Peter Nowell Jr. They were neighbors. I remember the Sanders family. They lived just a short distance on the trail from Grandpa Daniel's house.

According to his nephew, Buster Nowell said, "My uncle John Sanders was a surveyor, a brick layer and a carpenter. He built many homes on James Island. One home that I remember was the home of Miss Darlin Middleton [Ellen Middleton] on Grimball Road. In his spare time, he was also a farmer."

Abraham Sanders (1916) and his wife Florence Smalls (1920) had seven children: Ruth, Naomi, Fred, Abraham, Martha, John and Katherine. Florence, as I recall, was a sweet person. Her nickname was "Tootsie." She always had a smile on her face and had something good to say to you and would always ask how your family was doing. Years later they moved from the Turkey Pen area to the Secessionville Road area.

Daphne Sanders (1888), a widower, had one son, William Seymour (1915); three daughters, Mary Leise Seymour (1916), Anna Robinson (1914) and Hannah Richardson (1904); one granddaughter, Martha Richardson (1923); and a grandson, Howard Richardson (1925).

William Seymour Sr. (1915) and his wife Ethel had six sons, William Jr., Will Rogers, Warren, Hazel, Hasco and Leonard; and three daughters, Christine, Louise and Yvonne.

Arthur Rivers (1895) and his wife Martha (Neely) Young Rivers (1897–1970) had three sons, Robert (Tanny), Benjamin (1917–1962) and Isaiah; and one daughter, Alice. I remember Ms. Rivers. She was the first woman ordained as an elder in the St. James Presbyterian Church throughout the 1950s, under the leadership of Reverend Marion Sanders. This was an era when it was not popular for women to be leaders in the church.

Prince Fleming (1855) and his wife Janey (1875) had two daughters, Rachel (1886) and Eliza (1886); and three sons, Paul (1895), Cyrus (1895) and John (1899).

Arthur Bolds (1905) and his wife Louisa Smalls (1908) had five sons, Francis, Arthur, Herbert Lee, Herman and George; and six daughters, Thelma, Lillie Mae, Anna, Rosa, Irma and Phyllis.

Mose Young (1898) and his wife Julia Chisolm Young (1902) had one son, George (1924); and four daughters, Mattie (1927), Anna (1928), Elizabeth and Mildred. Julia Chisolm was the daughter of Morris Chisolm of the Grimball Plantation.

James Roper (1884) and his wife Irene (1889) had one son, James Jr. (1912); and four daughters, Percile (1913), Virginia (1916), Florence (1918) and Ruth (1927).

George Russell (1880), a widower, had three daughters, Mena (1908), Irene (1910) and Lilly (1915); and two sons, Franklin (1917) and Moses (1903).

Jacob Farr (1851) and his wife Rebecca (1870) had two daughters, Affy (1888) and Hester (1893); three sons, William (1890), John (1896) and James (1898); and a granddaughter, Minnie (1921); all were listed as mulattos.

Jessie Bonaparte (1852) and his wife Phyllis (1855–1918) had four sons, Hezekiah (1883), Ezekiel (1887), Jesse (1888) and Jenkins (1898); and two daughters, Dianna (1890) and Sylva (1892). Jessie's sister, Suzy (1891), was also living with him. The Bonapartes are all buried in the Burn Church cemetery.

James Grant (1866) and his wife Rebecca (1871) had one son, Joseph (1912). Living with the family was James's brother, Cyrus, and niece, Sarah Dawson (1885). James and Rebecca Grant were listed among the early members of Payne Church under the leadership of Reverend Pappy White.

Edward Grant (1892) and his wife Rebecca (1900) had three sons, Edward (1916), James (1922) and Isaac (1911); and two daughters, Rosa (1924) and Flora (1929).

Oley Brown (1901) and his wife Martha (1905) had three daughters, Emily (1925), Etta (1927) and Evelyn (1929). Oley was a farmer and farmed the area in the Fergerson Village. According to Joe Deleston, Oley had a mule named Mary, and he worked on his farm for a while.

Charles Knightly (1820) was married to Maria (1822). Living with them was Charles's father, Charles Knightly Sr. (1795), and a boarder, Eddie Williams (1849). Charles was one of the black state constables and one of the first of two black Democrats who were registered voters on James Island during the 1800s.

Joseph Simmons (1845) and his wife Sarah (1850) had three daughters, Maria (1878), Mary (1880) and Estel (1891); and three sons, Dick (1882), Eddie (1893) and Ellis 1895).

Samuel Simmons (1893) and his wife Bertha (1901) had two daughters, Corrine (1920) and Albertha (1929); and one son, Walter (1916). Also living in the household was Rebecca Flowers (1880), Samuel's sister in-law; Rebecca raised Richard Simmons (1923).

Hector Washington (1866) and his wife Rebecca (1880) had three daughters, Sarah (1893), Lucia (1896) and Maggie (1901); and one son, Christopher (1899). Their grandson, Richard Simmons (1923), was also living with them.

Richard Simmons (1923) and his wife Florence Todd (1924–2005) had five sons, Robert, Ronnie, Michael, Paul and Richard Jr.; and one daughter, Deborah. Richard retired from Westvaco Chemical Corporation after working for more than thirty years. He was a member and an elder at St. James Presbyterian Church. He was also one of the original members of the Sons of Elijah Masonic Lodge #457.

John (Guy) Simmons (1901) and his wife Maggie (1902) had three sons, Harry (1922), Richard 1923 and Andrew (1926); and two daughters, Phyllis (1925) and Estel (1929).

Willie Simmons (1886) and his wife Evelyn (1895) had two sons, Willie (1915) and Robert (1918); and five daughters, Lucile (1921), Irene (1922), Sylvia, Ethyl (1926) and Sarah (1929).

Hezekiah Simmons (1899) and his wife Sarah (1901) had three daughters, Wilhelmina (1919), Elizabeth (1920) and Sadie (1923); and two sons, Nehemiah (1925) and Hezekiah (1927).

Ellis Simmons (1900) and his wife Maria (1908) had one son, Expert (1928); also living with the family was a niece, Maybell Deleston (1922).

Peter Smith (1873) and his wife Josephine (1877) had four sons, Horace (1897), Rutledge (1899), Tom (1913) and D. (1915); and one daughter, Alina Smith (1905); all were mulattos.

John (Nat) Smith (1888) and his wife Liza (1890) had two sons, John (1910) and James (1927); and three daughters, Emily (1911), Melvina (1913) and Anna (1913). The latter two girls were twins.

Walter Hezekiah (1927) and his wife Etta Smalls (1927) had six daughters, Sarah Mae, Virginia, Evangeline, Beverly, Rosetta and Maxine; and three sons, Walter Jr., Curtis C. and Eric Hezekiah.

David (King) Smalls (1900) and his wife Rosa Grant (1902–1978) had five daughters, Ernestine (1921), Etta (1927), Rosa Lee (1929), Arolese (1930) and Shirley; and three sons, David Jr. (1924), Benjamin and Tona.

John Goss Sr. (1877) and his wife Amelia (1888) had four daughters, Florence (1913), Mary L. (1915), Elizabeth (1921) and Katharine (1921); and two sons, Horace (1905) and John Jr. (1917). John Goss Sr. is buried in the Dill cemetery.

Horace Goss (1905) and his wife Esther (1906) had ten sons, Benjamin, Horace (1921), Samuel (1924), James, Harold, Francis, Thomas (1929), William Henry, George Edward and Herman; and one daughter, Barbara Goss Brown.

Samuel "Sam" Goss (1924) and his wife Essline Champagne (1923) had seven daughters, Doris Champagne, Bertha Champagne, Carolyn Goss, Martha Goss, Janet Goss, Cheryl Goss and Edith Goss; and three sons, Samuel Goss Jr., Ronald Goss and Remus.

Edward "Moss" Drayton (1878) and his wife Louise Tindel had two sons, Rogers and Arthur; and five daughters, Dorothy Drayton Simmons (1911), Sarah, Ethel, Beatrice and Kerzel Drayton Fleming (1924).

CONVERSATIONS WITH KERZEL DRAYTON FLEMING

Kerzel Drayton Fleming (1924) was married to Prince Fleming (1922). During several conversations with Kerzel, she said,

> *Frazier, when I was a young girl, my family lived on Peach Grove Hill. It was a little further up on Flint Street from where I lived today. There was a lot of peach and pear trees on that place where we live called "The Hill." People called my daddy Moss Drayton, but his name was Edward. All roads on James Island were dirt roads when I was young.*
>
> *There was a dairy farm on the Dill Plantation where the senior citizens center is now located on Riverland Drive, called Birch Wood. The dairy was run by a man named McGinnis. My father would buy milk by the jugs for our family from the farm. Not far from our house was a hall on Central Park Road, called Central Park Hall. The older people in the community used the hall for their prayer meetings on Tuesday and Thursday evenings.*
>
> *There was a bell in the Lodge Hall, one in the hall on Riverland Drive and one in Bethel Church's steeple. When someone in the community died, a member of the deceased family let the secretary of the Lodge Hall know. He would ring*

Kerzel Drayton Fleming. *Family photograph.*

the bell until everyone got the news of the death. Sometime the people would have the undertaker bring their loved ones body to the hall until the time of burial.

The hall was used by the older people to have dances and have fun. The young children were not allowed to attend affairs with grownup. The hall was separated for recreations for the young children. On certain Sundays and holidays, the men and women would churn and make ice cream for us. Mama and Daddy would tell us when we went to the hall, they were going to spit on the ground at sundown and we should not let the spit dry before we get home because they would be waiting with a belt. When we noticed the sun going down, my sister and I started heading home.

I went to Cut Bridge Elementary School. The school was sitting in the marsh, on Stono Road, right next to the bridge where Riverland Drive and Camp Road intersect today. There was a store at that intersection call Tucker Store. The students would use they two-cent allowance to buy Johnnycake, sometimes called horse cake.

When I came of age, I married Prince Fleming, and got a job doing domestic work for several white families on James Island. This was the only kind of work a black woman could get besides working on the farms. I worked two days a week for the Glovers and also raised their two children. I works three days a week for Wade Sweatman in the Harborview Road area. Wade worked for the Charleston Naval Shipyard. My brother, Roger Drayton, worked in the same pipe fitter's shop where Mr. Sweatman works.

My husband got a job working for Bradham Construction Company paving the roads on James Island. They would mix hot tar and rock to pave the roads. Later, Prince got a job with Davis and Docher Construction, doing the same type of work, but they paid him a little bit more money. Son, I seen a lot of changes in my eighty years on this earth; I hope I live to see many more but that is up to the good Lord how long he sees fit for me to live.

Sandy "Samuel" Brown (1843) and his wife Betsy (1846) had one daughter, Patty (1859), and a son, Samuel Jr. (1869); both were listed as mulattos. According to historian records, Sandy Brown was one of the slaves who was granted forty acres by the Freedmen's Bureau and set up by the government in the 1800s on McLeod Plantation.

The land is located behind the Meridian Home Complex, at the end of Turkey Pen, on the Dill Plantation. This property is the only known land that was given to slaves on the Dill Plantation during this era that was not taken and returned to the plantation owners. Somehow, Sandy was able to hold onto the land and it is still listed in the tax office as the heirs of Sandy Brown, in care of Evelyn Nowell White, who lives in New York. Some of his descendants still live on the property as of this writing. One is a friend of mine, Buster Nowell.

Smiley Brown (1845) and his wife Grace (1872) had two daughters, Virginia (1896) and Clarinda (Christina) (1898); and four sons, Peter (1895), Joseph (1902), James (1904) and Elias (1908).

Another row of slave cabins was located approximately a mile from the first set of cabins. These cabins stretched from the southern part of Riverland Drive and ended up behind the shopping center at the Food Lion near Folly Road. They stood on the north side in front of the tall fortified battery. The battery was mounted with sand and stood approximately twenty feet high and about fifty feet wide and had a trench to the bottom. It stretched from the Stono River through Stono Road, through the Dill Plantation, where it intersected at Grimball Road and Riverland Drive.

There the battery crossed Folly Road as it intersected with Fort Johnson Road, which was previously Quarantine Road, through the area where the Westchester subdivision is now located. Then it stretched across Secessionville Road, which was previously old Savannah Road, to Battery Island Drive, and on to the end of Sol Legare Road to the Stono River. Many parts of the battery stayed intact during my early teen years until the 1980s.

The battery was constructed by slave labor. It was used by Confederate soldiers to protect and defend Charleston from the Union army during the Civil War. According to history, the shot that started the Civil War was fired from Fort Sumter in Charleston harbor. The war began on April 12, 1861, and ended April 9, 1865.

Sefus Todd (1819) and his wife Emma (1822) had two sons, Peter (1844) and Charles (1855). Peter Todd (1844) and his wife Lilly (1844) had three daughters, Lucy (1858), Emma (1888) and Celia (1892); two sons, Joe (1882) and Primus; and a grandson, Eugene. Peter also fathered a daughter with Rosa Ann Pinckney, Ethel Pinckney Todd. Peter Todd is listed among the foundering fathers of Payne RMUE Church on Camp Road in 1875.

71

Joe Todd (1882) and his wife Alice (1887) had four daughters, Josephine (1910), Eselin (1912), Alice (1914) and Florence (1923); two sons, Joseph (1921) and John Henry (1923); and a granddaughter, Edith Heyward (1925).

Alexander Mikell and his wife Ethel (1913) had five daughters, Bernice (1929), Anna Lee (1930), Ethel (1934), Bertha Lee (1936) and Elouise; and one son, Alexander Jr.

John Heyward (1885) and his wife Elouise (1887) had one son, Edward (1906); one daughter, Sarah (1908); and an adopted son, Alonzo Roper (1920).

John Smalls (1850) and his wife Jane (1855) had one daughter, Carrie Drayton (1893); one son, Edward Drayton (1899); and two granddaughters, Phyllis Drayton (1905) and Essie Drayton (1906). John's mother, Peggy Brown (1830), was also living with the family.

James Brown and his wife Alice Todd Brown (1914–2004) had three sons, Nathaniel, Erwin and James Jr.; and five daughters, Carol, Mary, Florence, Louise and Elma Brown.

Jeffery Heyward (1900) and his wife Diana Todd Heyward (1907) had two daughters, Edith and Frances; and two sons, James and Herman.

Thomas Middleton (1808) and his wife Flora (1825) had one daughter, Daphine (1855); and one son, Jimmie (1858); all were mulattos. According to information passed down through oral history and research, Flora Middleton (1825), Mary Smalls (1830) and Daniel Hard left for Africa in 1877.

According to several slaves, the three had saved for years with the idea of going to Africa, their ancestors' home. After several years in Africa, they returned to Charleston in 1890; according to Ms. Middleton, they were disillusioned at what they saw concerning living conditions in Africa.

Thomas Middleton (1858) and his wife Rachel Pinckney Middleton had three sons, Irving (1916), Thomas (1919) and Herbert Remus (1922); and three daughters, Essie (1914), Bernetha (1919) and Janie Middleton.

Thomas Middleton (1919) and his wife Theresa M. (1924) had two sons, Thomas M. and Rogers E.; and one daughter, Gloria. In my conversations with Thomas, he said,

> *Frazier, my aunt Janie raised my brothers, sisters and me. I left Charleston in 1940, during World War II, and joined the U.S. Navy. At the end of the war, I ended up living in Boston, Massachusetts. When I was a young boy, I used to caddy for white men on the golf course in Charleston and became interested in the sport. There were no golf courses for blacks in Charleston, and segregation was rigidly enforced in the South.*
>
> *I became associated with the Franklin Park Golf Course in the 1950s, while living in Boston, and competed in tournaments throughout the region, occasionally traveling as far as Miami.*

In 1958, Thomas Middleton became the first African American to win the championship at the course. He repeated as champion the following year, after playing the course for over a decade. The turmoil of the 1960s brought Franklin Park Golf Course to the brink of extinction.

Thomas and a group consisting of about a dozen golfers, known as the Franklin Park Golf Club Group, maintained the golf course, mowed the lawns and ran the clubhouse. According to an article written, there was a rebirth. Thomas and his group paved the way for young male African Americans' involvement in the sport, decades before Tiger Woods and other recognized Africans Americans ventured on the scene. After he retired, Thomas and his beautiful wife returned home to South Carolina, where he lived on James Island, the place where he was born and raised. Thomas and his wife are members of St. James Presbyterian Church.

Janie Middleton Murray (1880), a widow and a schoolteacher, had one daughter, Clara Smalls (1925). Living in her household were her three brothers, Irving Middleton (1916), Thomas Middleton (1919) and Herbert Remus Middleton (1922), as well as her two sisters, Esse Middleton (1914) and Bernetha Middleton (1919).

The last section of this historical fortified battery at Riverland Drive and Folly Road was pushed down to build the Pantry Store, the Hess Mart Store and the credit union. However, sections of the battery can still be seen in the wooded areas on Riverland Drive across from where the Carolina Sky Way Airport once stood across the road from King Solomon Lodge Hall on the Dill Plantation.

I remember some of the people living in these slave cabins in front of the tall battery on the north side. Many died decades before I was born, but evidence of their existence and legacy lives on.

Barstow Brown (1835) and his wife Mena (1855) had two sons, Henry (1884) and Joseph (1881). Joseph Brown was a mulatto; the census lists him as being the son of plantation owner Joseph Dill. According to Harry Urie, his grandfather, Hump, said that Joseph Dill fathered several children with women slaves. The 1900 census supports his claim that Joseph Dill is the father of Joseph Brown.

Joseph Brown (1881) was married to Louisa Brown (1881).

Jeffery Lemon (1910–1984) and his wife Sadie Ladson Lemon (1910) had two sons, Jeffery Jr. and McArthur; and seven daughters, Martha, Mary, Janie, Sarah, Patsy, Ruth and Masline.

CONVERSATIONS WITH JEFFERY LEMON

Everyone in the community affectionately called Jeffery "Mr. Jeffery." Years before he died, I had numerous conversations with him. During these conversations he said,

> Son, I moved in the slave house in front of the tall battery after Boy Smith and his wife Anna Smith moved out. The slaves that stayed there before them died long before that. I was the foreman for Park Mikell after he took over running the plantation from "Old Man King."
>
> When time comes to pick the string beans, we put them in bushel baskets and potatoes in two-hundred-pound bags during the late 1930s through 1960s, I paid the peoples twenty-five cent a bushel for string beans and fifteen cents for two hundred pounds of potatoes on order from Mr. Park. I think the pay was raised in 1948, or 1949, to fifity cents a bushel for string beans, and twenty-five cent for a two-hundred-pound bag of Irish potatoes.

Jeffery Lemon. *Family photograph.*

Most times I paid the peoples at the end of each day picking string beans and Irish potatoes. Sometimes I would give them token in place of money. They would cash the token on Friday for cash money. I knew to myself that the people deserved more money than we paid them, but what the hell could you do, Park was the boss!

Son there was some hella of time working for Park. One thing about him he had no respect for black peoples. I remember many days when my son-in-law, Nay [Joe Deleston], Lonzo [Alonzo Moore] and Albert were driving tractors on the farm. He would raise hell, cursing, ranting and raving about them boys running the tractor full speed plowing up potatoes; then get in my case for letting them do it. He did not pay me a decent salary, but I made up for that in other ways; I think you know what I mean.

Mr. Jeffery grinned; I knew what he meant. I was a young boy working on the farm picking beans and bagging potatoes during Mr. Jeffery's period as a foreman.

The slave cabin where Mr. Jeffery lived was on the Old Stono Road, in front of the tall battery. The road ran near the entrance to the Carolina Sky Way Airport. Mr. Jeffery would later move his family to a house that he built at the intersection of Riverland Drive and Grimball Road, in front of the Civil War battery next to Charles Whaley's property.

That part of the battery was eventually leveled during the 1970s. Mr. Jeffery was never given a deed to the property by the plantation's owner. After all of his children were of age, he and his wife, Sadie, moved to a residential home on Johns Island. His oldest son, Jeffery Lemon Jr., and daughter, Janie Lemon, and I grew up together.

Arthur Champagne (1896) and his wife Estel Roper Champagne (1897–2003) had one son, Arthur Jr. (1929), and three daughters, Rosa Lee (1919), Esalina (1923) and Arsolee (Moutsie). The young people in the community called him Mr. Arta, and his wife Ms. Dell. They were also farmers on the plantation. He had a one-room small board building with a door and no window that was used as a store on Riverland Drive.

The store was located diagonally across the road from King Solomon Lodge Hall on Riverland Drive. During the 1940s and the early 1950s, everyone in the community would patronize his little store; the people loved those link sausages he sold in his store for ten cents.

Arthur and his wife, along with the majority of the older men and women on the island, enjoyed smoking their pipe; sometimes he also smoked cigars. After the death of Mr. Arthur Champagne Sr., his son Arthur Jr., moved his mother, Ms. Dell, back to her parents' property on Grimball Road, then to his sister's house. He took care of her every need until her death in 2003. She lived to be one hundred years old.

Richard (Manny) Champagne (1889–1936) and his wife Virginia Brown (1896–1963) had six daughters, Elizabeth (1915), Melvina "Blossom" (1918), Mary (1921), Florence (1923), Sarah (1926) and Virginia (1927). Florence married Harry Urie, and they moved to Fergerson Village. All of the children in the community, including myself, called Mrs. Virginia by her nickname, "Cun Mama." Her house was one of the places where we played as kids near the battery.

Louis Gladden (1873) and his wife Pigeon had two sons, Willie (1906) and Abraham (1900). After the death of his wife, Louis moved to Grimball Road, where he married Livinia Smalls, who was also a widow.

Willie Gladden (1906) and his wife Lena Burden Gladden (1908) had four sons, Louis (1928), Thomas (1927), William (1929) and Henry (1932); and two daughters, Lillian and Ethel. After the death of Lena, Willie married his second wife. They had two sons, Thomas and Phillip. Willie Gladden was one of those men who also loved to smoke his pipe.

Joe Gladden (1905) and his wife Marylee (1906) had one daughter, Clara, and a son, George. Joe raised Susan Lemon, his sister in-law. She later married my uncle, James Smalls. Joe and his family lived in the last cabin next to the shopping center that was later built at Riverland Drive and Folly Road.

William Ladson (1880) and his wife Matilda (1881) had five daughters, Nellie (1904), Matilda (1907), Mary (1909), Julia (1913) and Lizzie (1915); and two sons, James (1911) and George (1916).

James Jenkins (1883) and his wife Mariah (1888) had five sons, Cesar (1912), Moses (1913), Elijah (1918), Joseph (1920) and Leroy. James Jenkins and his family were also sharecroppers and farmers on the Dill Plantation until the late 1940s, when he packed his family and moved to Johns Island.

Archie Jenkins (1865) and his wife Josephine (1865) had two daughters, Josephine (1884) and Hester (1888); and two sons, James (1883) and Caleb (1895).

Runty Gathers (1872) and his wife Hester (1875) had two daughters, Elouise Rivers (1892) and Maggie Rivers (1905); and two sons, William Rivers (1901) and Elias Rivers (1898), all mulattos.

Ezekiel Gathers (1885) and his wife Martha (1890) had two sons, Isaac (1908) and Ezekiel (1921); and two daughters, Evelina (1915) and Rebecca (1916). Also living in the house were daughter-in-law Elizabeth (1905); two granddaughters, Maltilda (1926) and Ruthe (1929); and a grandson, Oscar (1923).

Frank Gathers (1893) and his wife Julia (1902) had four sons, Frankie (1917), Leroy (1921), John (George) H. (1926) and Elias (1918); and three daughters, Patsy (1915), Mary A. (1920) and Florrie (1926). After moving to the city of Charleston, George Gathers was among the first group of black police officers hired with the City of Charleston, in 1950.

April Washington (1860) and his wife Annie (1862) had five sons, Joseph (1880), Isaac (1883), Abraham (1885), Cuffie (1895) and April (1889); and two daughters, Rina (1890) and Julia (1894). Also living with the family was granddaughter Lillie Belle Allen (1915) and grandson Benjamin Allen (1916).

There were many other slaves' cabins scattered throughout that area but they were old, rotted and abandoned by slaves that had died or moved away decades before I was born.

When I was around ten years old, several of us in the community would play on the Civil War battery, including Leon Deleston (1935), Clarence Gibbs (1936), Jackie Todd (1936), Samuel Gathers (1936), Ernest Middleton (1936), Leroy Jenkins and Thomas Smalls (1936). We would crawl and climb to the top of the tall battery and then slide back down to the bottom. We considered this a sporting event.

The people living in the slaves' cabins would yell at us, "Yu all com don fron top da hill, yu har." They would then inform our parents. There were several locations on the battery in front of those cabins where we would play. However, this adventure came to an end as several of us went home with torn pants and the beatings that we received sealed this period of adventure in our lives. In retrospect, all of my friends listed above are now deceased with the exception of my cousin, Thomas Smalls.

Peter Bryan (1812), a widower, had three daughters, Eleanor (1844), Lucy (1847) and Dolly (1857); and one son, John (1852). Also living with the family were his brother and sister, Thomas (1824) and Laura (1831).

In order to reach the Grimball Plantation on Riverland Drive by foot, you would pass the cotton fields that Carolina Sky Way Airport once occupied, then King Solomon Lodge Hall with several houses along the way during slavery and throughout the farming era.

In the first house lived Samson Duxein (1820) and his wife Moria Duxein (1825). They had three daughters, Pauline Duxein Smalls, Elizabeth Duxein Miller and Mary Duxein Todd.

Charleston County Court records revealed that Samson Duxein bought twenty acres of land from Joseph T. and Regina A. Dill for the sum of $400 on June 8, 1883, and recorded in the RMC Office on June 25, 1883. Many of Samson's descendants still live on the property adjacent to King Solomon Lodge Hall. The deed is still recorded in the name of the heirs of Samson Duxien.

Primus Todd (1894) and his wife Mary Duxein (1898) had five sons, Willis, Primus Jr. (1917), Harold (1923), Richard (1929) and Jackie (1936); and five daughters, Elizabeth (1915), Helen (1919), Bertha (1921), Lulie (1925) and Catharine (1922). Mary moved her family from McColl Woods, after the death of her husband, to her parents' property on Riverland Drive.

Mary owned a small farm and planted and harvested vegetables to sell at the market in Charleston. She also raised chickens and hogs to support her family. She was my mother's aunt. Everyone in the family called her Aunt Lillie; her son Jackie and I grew up together.

Frank Richardson (1917) and his wife Helen Todd (1919) had one son, Frank Jr.; and two daughters, Deloris and Lorraine. During conversations with Helen, she said,

> *Son, I was born in that area known as McColl Wood. My father, Primus Todd, farmed there. He grows all kinds of vegetables. During harvest season, he would load his wagon, hitch his horse up and drive to Charleston. There he would sell his vegetables to stores that would buy from him.*
>
> *When I was six years old, my mother sent me to live with my aunt, Hester Miller. She used to live right here on this property where we live now. I helped take care of her daughter Lucile. She was my first cousin. I was older than her. I married my husband Frank in 1946; he got a job working at the Charleston Naval Shipyard and work until he retired.*

Louis Miller (1855) and his wife Elizabeth Duxein Miller (1875) had two daughters, Emma Miller Smalls (1894) and Hester (Hesse) Miller (1909); and one son, Robert (1900).

Hester (Hesse) Miller (1909) had one daughter, Lucile (1924). Hesse was also a farmer and raised chickens and hogs, as the other farmers did on the island. Her grandson, Larry Backman, did most of her work, such as plowing the fields and feeding the hogs and chickens.

George Glover (1923–1975) and his wife Lucile (1924) had two daughters, Deborah and Georgetta; and two sons, Larry Backman and Ray Glover.

Joseph Gathers (1911–1959) and his wife Charlotte Johnson (1909–1990) had four sons, William Scott (1929), Samuel (1936), Edward and Joseph; and three daughters, Charlotte, Hannah and Mary. Living with Joseph, according to the 1930s census reports, was his grandmother, Hannah Gathers (1836).

Samuel Johnson Sr. (1865) and his wife Hanna Gadsden (1868) had four sons, Edward (1908), Peter (1912), Samuel Jr. (1906) and Isaac (1915); one daughter, Charlotte (1909); and a grandson, William Scott (1929).

Truman Cromwell (1854) and his wife Cloranda (1855) had two sons, Allen (1870) and William (1878); and five daughters, Rosa (1880), Gallie, Isabella (1882), Julia (1884) and Raddie (1888). According to the minutes from St. James Presbyterian Church in 1868, Truman was one of several former slaves who carried lumber on his shoulders, walking from the Seabrooks' boat landing at Wappoo Creek along Secessionville Road, some two and a half miles to the corners of Fort Johnson and Secessionville Roads. There the first black Presbyterian church was built under the leadership of Reverend H. Hunter in 1868.

Allen Cromwell Sr. (1870) and his wife Christine (1875) had two sons, Allen Jr. (1920) and Samuel (1924); and one daughter, Essie. Allen Cromwell Sr. was a member of King Solomon Lodge Hall. His son Samuel Cromwell is married to Mary Frazier Cromwell, my father's sister.

In 1863, President Abraham Lincoln signed the Emancipation Proclamation freeing the slaves. However, it would be over a century in the South before African Americans realized any relief from this action. Grandpa said, "Afa da wod waz pass ron dey waz fee, we ha tu pey Massa to tay on fam or gu." (After the slaves learned they were free they had to sharecrop to pay the master for rent or leave the plantation.)

According to Grandpa and Hump Urie Sr., most of them had no money to buy the land, so they had to sharecrop. History would later corroborate and substantiate my grandpa's statement. Even though Joseph Dill trusted my grandfather with his family and used him as his personal chauffeur on the plantation his entire life, they gave him nothing.

There is no known record that slaves were given deeds to property on the Dill Plantation by the owner for their hard work, decades of loyalty and sacrifice. According to Grandpa, Joseph Dill promised him and his brother-in-law Peter Todd and Hump Urie deeds to the property where they were living in 1890.

Joseph Dill died in 1900, before giving them deeds to the property. His daughters refused to honor that promise. Instead the land was deeded as a wildlife refuge by his daughters, Pauline and Julia Dill. Decades later, the land was developed as a housing complex where the Meridian subdivision now stands on Riverland Drive.

While he did not say what year or on which plantation, Grandpa said that his pa told him a black man came to the slave cabins at night trying to get some of the men on the plantation to help "Bun don Chusn un ded da Massa." (Burn down Charleston and kill the slave master.) His father did not say if any of the slaves went with the man. "Da mon wa cath hugtic un ded." (The men were caught, hanged and died.) As a young boy at the time, I did not place any significance concerning these conversations.

It would be five decades after the death of my grandfather and my researching of history that I realized he had to have been talking about Denmark Vesey, or one of his trusted lieutenants. According to historical records, Denmark Vesey was born in Africa or Haiti, but as a boy was raised in St. Thomas in the Virgin Islands.

He traveled on a ship as a slave boy with Captain Joseph Vesey. Historical records show him having no known formal education. Yet, as an adult, he could speak and write in English. Vesey was a carpenter by trade and purchased his freedom working as a carpenter in a lottery he won in Charleston.

According to historical records, Denmark Vesey lived in Charleston for forty years, with the last twenty-two of those years as a freedman at 20 Bull Street in Charleston. This location is reportedly where, in 1822, he organized the insurrection to overthrow the white slave masters and made plans to kill them, including women and children, and burn down Charleston. Through his lieutenants, Vesey recruited men from the surrounding plantations that he considered trustworthy.

It appears that Vesey planned this insurrection with the utmost secrecy among the slaves he selected. He was careful not to trust slaves that were called "house niggers" and those that were half-white. This insurrection would have succeeded, according to documentation, if it were not for one of his lieutenants who recruited a "house nigger" he trusted, who betrayed Vesey and his loyal followers. The insurrection was discovered and Vesey and thirty-five of his followers were hanged.

It was shortly after Vesey was hanged that vigilantes caught three runaway slaves, a male, female and a young child. All were killed but in addition, the man was decapitated and his head was stuck on a pole and publicly exposed as a "warning to other slaves!"

THE GRIMBALL
PLANTATION OWNERS

PAUL CHAPLIN GRIMBALL (1645) AND his wife Mary had one son, Thomas H. (1682), who was married to Joyce Grimball. The following are descendants of Paul and Thomas H. Grimball. Henry Grimball (1860–1943) was married to Lula P. Grimball (1864–1952). Raymond Grimball (1887–1967) was married to Beulah Grimball (1889–1978). Burmain A. Grimball (1895–1957) was married to Violet D. Grimball (1893–1979).

The Grimball Plantation stretched along the bank of the Stono River, from the Dill Plantation to Grimball Road East, to Stono Road (now Riverland Drive), to Folly Road; then south to Grimball Road, to the Sol Legare Plantation. The Grimballs' houses were built along the bank of the Stono River.

The slave schedule from 1850 to 1860 shows the Grimball family owned 195 slaves, including 15 known mulattos, during these years.

The archive in Charleston houses the last will and testament of Paul Chaplin Grimball. It stated in part, "I, Paul Chaplin Grimball in the State aforesaid do hereby make and declare this to be my last Will and Testament."

In his will, Mr. Grimball acknowledges purchasing twenty-seven slaves from Charles J. Steadman, sheriff of Charleston District, on February 6, 1832; he also bought eight slaves from James M. Croskey and Richard Teasdale on March 5, 1832, which raised his total number to about sixty slaves.

In the third section of his will Mr. Grimball stated, "I give and bequeath to my son Thomas H. Grimball his heirs and assign forever my plantation on James Island in the Parish of St. Andrews, known as 'Waverly' including all my land on said island together with one third part of all my Negro 'slaves.'"

In the fourth section of the will, Mr. Grimball stated,

> I bequeath to my sons, Isaac P. Grimball and Thomas H. Grimball, my tract of land on John Island known as "Waterloo" and the tract of pine land belonging to it for fencing and firewood containing together about one thousand acres and the following Negroes slaves. [Thirty-eight slaves were here listed by first name.]

Cotton shed on the Grimball Plantation on the bank of the Stono River. *Family photograph.*

Further to Maria a present from her brother, Thomas, together with one third of my house and yard Negroes to be held in trust for my daughter Pauline. The said tract of land and Negro slaves being intended to be set apart as a fund for certain support of my daughter Pauline and her children.

Signed sealed by Testator Paul Chaplin Grimball. LS

Witness

Kinsey Burden, Paul T. Gervais Jr., C.J. Whaley

Probate in common form George Buist, Esq.

Ordinary Charleston District on the eighteen day of August Anno Domino 1864, on the second day of January 1865, qualified Isaac P. Grimball Executor therein named—Ex; G.B.

SLAVES AND THEIR DESCENDANTS RESIDING ON THE GRIMBALL PLANTATION

At the intersection of Grimball Road where it intersects with Riverland Drive, I recall the first house on the Grimball Plantation beginning on the south side of the small one-lane dirt road headed south. It was the home of Charles Whaley.

Charles Whaley (1889–1967) and his wife Sarah Milton (1895–1944) had five sons, Charles Henry (1917), Samuel (1921), Benjamin (1923), Nathaniel (1925) and Remus (1927); and one daughter, Ruby (1928). After the death of his first wife Sarah, Charles met and married Irene Blossom Green in 1945; Charles was a farmer and a deacon at St. James Presbyterian Church.

CONVERSATIONS WITH RUBY WHALEY BELLENGER

Ruby Whaley Bellenger (1928–2004) and her husband Herbert Bellenger had four sons, Herbert Jr., Charles Albert, Bernard James and Johnathan Harris; and four daughters, Brenda Bernice Randolph, Paula Spring Bellenger, Sherry Ann Gallashaw and Arthurine Angela Bellenger.

Ruby, the daughter of Charles and Sarah Whaley, was a minister and resided on the same property that her father once lived on and owned. She had a church next door to her residence on the same property. During our interview, Ruby said,

> *Son, my grandpa, Henry Whaley Sr. [1862–1930] and his wife, Peggy, bought ten acres of land near the Stono River from the Grimballs for $70. He gave that property to his two sons, Elias and Enoch Whaley. Their descendants still live there today. He gave my father this property where I live today.*
>
> *Did you know it was a tradition of black folks during the 1900s, through the 1940s when there were no telephones, they would relay messages by drum in the community. If someone was sick, or died you would hear the sound of drumbeats, boom, boom, boom, for several moments up to an hour.*
>
> *Upon hearing the drum, my father would send my brother, Ben, riding the horse in the direction the sound was coming from to find out what happened or who died. This was how the peoples communicate since there was no telephone. No matter what time day or night the drum would let the community know.*
>
> *I remember Joseph Deleston Sr., Joe Frazier and Louis Gladden. They were the three men that beat the drum for King Solomon Lodge Hall during my years growing up. In fact, Joseph's first wife, Emily Deleston, was the last person I recall the drum beaten for. People would march behind the hearse to the cemetery. I never forget the Sunday my mother died in St. James Presbyterian Church of a heart attack. That day it seemed like my world came to an end. I guess there is no better place to die than in the church.*
>
> *Son, I been through a lot of trials and tribulation during my life. After I reached a certain point in my life, I turned everything over to God. As you well know I delved into His work, and through him I had this church built, Reform Church of Christ, where, as a minister, I have been serving him ever since.*

Mrs. Bellenger died six months after my interview with her in 2004.

I also remember that Sunday, December 17, 1944, that Mrs. Bellenger referred to. I was in church with my father when Mrs. Sarah Whaley died of an apparent heart attack in St. James Presbyterian Church.

Charles Henry Whaley Sr. (1917–1955), and his wife Catherine Smalls Whaley (1919–2001) had four sons, Charles Jr., Isaiah, Zenous and George; and five daughters, Mary, Catherine, Hester, Richardine and Laura.

I attended school with some of the Whaley children, Charles, Marie and Hester, during the early 1940s through 1950s. I was in high school when Charles Sr. and his wife Catherine packed up the family and moved to New York. There weren't many opportunities for blacks in the South. During the 1930s, '40s and throughout the 1970s, many blacks in Charleston were migrating north in search of a better life for their family. The Whaley family was among them.

This was during an era when blacks in the South were close even if they were not related by blood or marriage. I was young at the time and must admit that I hated to see the Whaley family leave. I knew they left Charleston hoping to make a better life for their family. I guess because of the attachment and tradition between families and friends it left a void in the community.

I recall that on many occasions, my friends Clarence Gibbs, Leon Deleston, Sam Gathers (all deceased now) and I would visit the Whaley house. We would sit on their porch in pretense of visiting Charles Jr., our friend. We called him by his nickname, Pork. However, in reality, our visit to Charles was so that we could see and admire his sisters. Of course, we did not fool Mr. Whaley. He also had a nickname, "Big Mog." He would be in his yard working on cars and give us that look out of the corner of his eyes and say, "Mind, boys."

Prior to migrating to New York, Mr. Whaley did auto mechanic work at his residence and was very good. On numerous occasions, my mother would send me to Ms. Catherine's house when she needed some sewing done. Ms. Catherine was one of the seamstresses in the community.

Prince (Princy) White (1866) and his wife Sarah (1882) had three daughters, Emmy, Irene and Wilhmenia. Wilhmenia is listed as mulatto. They also had a grandson, Prince Richardson, living with the family.

Prince was a farmer who also raised hogs to sell, grew sugar cane, pears, figs and pecan trees in his yard. I recall many people in the community, including my family, bought sticks of sugar cane and pecans from him. He owned and rode a red horse with a saddle on the Grimball section of James Island during my teenage years.

Although Prince was a farmer on the Grimball Plantation, he was raised on the Seabrook Plantation with four brothers and his father, Pappy White, a slave and overseer on the Seabrook Plantation. According to my grandma, Mary Chavis Frazier, Prince was one of the men injured during the 1893 storm.

Following the death of Prince and his wife Irene, they were buried in the slave cemetery on Secessionville Road located near the intersection of Camp Road, reserved for the slaves and their descendants of the Seabrook Plantation. Ronald Brown, grandson of Prince, said, "The last time I visited my grandparents' graves

Prince White and his wife, Sarah White. *Family photograph.*

to place flowers on them, developers had removed the headstone, and a house was built near the gravesite."

In 1984, this cemetery went on sale because of delinquent tax. When it was discovered that the developer was building on the cemetery graves, it was stopped by a group of citizens led by the Reverend Cornelius Campbell, pastor of St. James Presbyterian Church, and Thomas Johnson, president of the Westchester Community Civic Organization.

At a public auction held by the Charleston County Tax Office, Mrs. Rosalee Frazier Fergerson, secretary of the organization, placed a bid on the property to preserve it as a slave cemetery. However, she was outbid by a white male out of Mt. Pleasant, South Carolina. At this time, the cemetery remains in limbo with descendants unable to visit their ancestors' graves.

William Cromwell (1878) and his wife Tena (1879) had one daughter, Anna (1915); and two sons, Marion (1899) and Oscar (1911). After the death of Tena, William married his second wife, Mary Gladden Cromwell.

William Cromwell (1878) and his second wife Mary Gladden (1892) had five sons, Ernest (1918), Ellison (1924), William Jr., (1925), Herbert 1 (1928) and Leon; and three daughters, Betsy (1920), Mary Leise (1922) and Josephine (1933).

Alfred Richardson (1870) and his wife Rosa Cromwell Richardson (1880) had one daughter, Nellie (1920); and three sons, Elias (1918), Alfred Jr. (1922) and Edwin

(1929). The people in the community called Rosa "Cun Rosa"; I remember two of her sons, Alfred and Elias. Alfred Sr. was also one of the men on the Grimball Plantation who was hurt during the 1893 storm.

I was a teenager when I realized Alfred Jr. was blind. He was a quiet man; I used to enjoy talking with him. He would tell us stories about the old days as we sat around him on his mother's porch. The children called him by his nickname, Alf. Sometimes he would ask one of us to lead him down the dirt road while holding his cane as he followed behind to Old Man Frank Deleston's house, under the oak trees on Grimball Road. These large oak trees in Cousin Frank's yard were a hangout for people in the community.

Edger Middleton (1898) and his wife Ellen (1898) had four sons, Eddie, Herman, Ernest and James; and five daughters, Melvenia, Rosa Lee, Evelyn, Margaret and Teresa.

Samuel Roper Sr. (1871–1939) and his wife Elsey (1873–1950) had five daughters, Florine (1892), Estel (Dell) (1896–2003), Rebecca (1897), Rose (1898) and Mary (1899); and two sons, John (1901) and Samuel Jr. (1912). Elsey raised two granddaughters, Cecelia Simmons (1915) and Margaret Simmons; and one grandson, Joseph Simmons.

Sam Green (1914) and his wife Cecelia Simmons Green (1915) had four sons, Isaac Johnson, Edward, Ellis and James; and six daughters, Mattie, Carrie, Elizabeth, Mary, Barbara and Marcia.

CONVERSATIONS WITH CECELIA SIMMONS GREEN

During an interview, Cecelia said,

Son, I grew up in my grandma's house after my mama and daddy separated. She raised my sister, brother and me. When I was six years old, I had to work on the farms just like the rest of the children that lived on Grimball Plantation. My sister and me went with Grandma to pick cotton, potatoes, string beans, tomatoes and a lot of other vegetables, on most of the farms.

The Grimballs, Dills, Rivers, Clarks, Lawtons and Ellises are some of the farms I remember working on. During the early 1920s through the 1930s, I worked on the Dill farm picking cotton with your mother, Sis, your Aunt Child, Eva, Ethel and Emmy and Omega Deleston.

The Dills' cotton fields were in the same place where the airport used to be [Carolina Sky Way Airport], *next to the King Solomon Lodge Hall on Riverland Drive. I remember Mr. King who was running the Dill farm at the time. He paid one cent a pound to pick cotton. He was a nasty white man. Many times we heard him calling black people "nigger."*

The Grimballs' cotton field was near the Stono River, off Grimball Road close to their houses. They also farmed that area by the slave cemetery [Evergreen Cemetery] *where the James Island School and the Baxter Patrick School is today. The Grimballs paid two cents a pound to pick cotton. It sure took a long*

Cecelia Simmons Green. *Family photograph.*

time to pick a pound of cotton; during the school season, I went to Society Corner School on Secessionville Road.

I met my husband Sam Green, and we got married in 1938. We moved to the Lawton Bluff Plantation. We worked and lived on the farm. Mr. Lawton planted corn, cabbages, collard greens and strings beans. At the end of the farming season, Mr. Lawton would turn his cows and mules in the pasture to graze. Mr. Lawton had lot of jersey cows, you know, those black and white ones.

I also worked on the Mikell and Hinson farms while we lived on the Lawton Plantation. They also had cows; their cows was mostly brown and white. After the men milk the cows, my husband, Sam, was in charge of straining the milk on the farm and see that it was poured into those big milk jugs.

Mr. Arthur Scott was the driver of the horse and wagon on the Hinson and Mikell Plantations. He would take the milk to Lawton Bluff; Sam Gardener, the truck driver for the Lawton Plantation, would drive the milk to the West End Dairy in Charleston on President Street. Lota men in our neighborhood would go in the farmer's field on Friday night, and teaf corn, tomatoes, cabbages, string beans and collard greens. The wife would take it to Charleston on Saturday to sell at the market.

One day, a group of us were working in the field. We overheard Mr. Hinson talking to another white man; he was telling him, "You all think them niggers stupid, but they have plenty of sense. I think some of them been going in my fields at night stealing my vegetables and selling it on the market;" we would hold our head down and laugh at him because we knew who was teafing the vegetables.

After Mr. Lawton got sick, he begins selling his cows, mules and land to the black peoples that could afford to buy them. That when many of the black people move to Charleston and places throughout the county. They had to find place to lives. Some went north to New York.

After Mr. Lawton died, my husband and me moved back to my grandmother Elsey, on the Grimball Plantation. We stayed with her until my husband and me were able to build this house on Fort Johnson Road where I live today. Son, they was many days we worked twelve hours in the rain, the colds and the hot sun, but we made it this far by believing in God and praying.

Although there were hard times on James Island for the black people, we learn to survive. Some of the plantation owners were fairly decent to us. Mr. Ephraim Clark, Lawton and the Grimballs sell land to black peoples at reasonable price they could afford. The Seabrooks did give blacks the property where the Payne RMUE Church was built; the Dills gave the slaves nothing. But still, God was good to us through our hard work, pain and suffering. We kept the faith and pray he help us survived, Amen.

Richard Smalls Sr. and his wife Wilhelmina had six sons, Richard Jr., James, Clarence, Samuel, Harold and Ronald; and three daughters, Dorothy, Edith (Gladys) and Ernestine.

During the 1930s through the late 1960s, segregation was still being enforced in Charleston. Black men who were interested in the sport of golf had no course to play on other than carrying the white men's bags as a caddy. Their only hope was to drive the ball behind their house if the yard was large and long enough or in an open field if it wasn't being used by the farmers.

Richard Smalls Sr., a young black man who had spent many years on the Country Club Golf Course as a caddy for the white men, decided to do something about their predicament. Over the years, he studied blueprints and plans on how golf courses were built. Richard bought the eight acres of property that sit next to the Frazier property from Raymond Grimball. With his nephew, Harry Urie, a carpenter, they built the first part of the clubhouse and bar and named it Little Rock Golf Club.

Richard purchased a small Ford tractor and, with help from my brother Jimmy and many other men in the community, he cleared the land of trees and bushes and built a six-hole golf course. Black men were able to play golf on the course until the white Municipal Golf Course in Charleston was forced to integrate by the courts.

Samuel Matthews (1875) and his wife Nancy (1878) had one son, John (1900); and eleven daughters, Sarah (1896), Eliza (1898), Emma (1916), Elouise (1914), Janie (1905), Essie (1912), Tena, Melvena (1918), Bernice, Diana (1921) and Catharine (1922). After the death of her mother, Liza raised her siblings to adulthood.

Liza Matthews (1898) had two daughters, Willamae (1920) and Nancy (1927). According to Nancy, Liza started working as a maid for Henry and Lula Grimball when she was a young woman. After the death of Henry and Lula, she worked for Raymond Grimball until his death. Her father had a small farm that she worked on besides working for the Grimballs. After the death of her mother, Liza raised

Mary Chavis Frazier, author's paternal grandmother. *Family photograph.*

her siblings and moved from the area where she lived in the Pie House section to Grimball Road, next door to the Fraziers.

On the south side of the road lived my paternal great-great grandfather, Benjamin Frazier Sr. (1020), and his wife, Sibby (1030). They had three sons, Cyrus (1852), Ben (1871) and Robert Christopher (1874); and two daughters, Dolly (1852) and Phoebe Sylvia (1865). Cyrus and Dolly were twins.

Information passed down through oral history and research reveal that Benjamin was brought here as a slave from the west coast of Africa. Benjamin was sold to the Grimball Plantation, where he met and married Sibby Royal. According to family members, Phoebe, the daughter of Benjamin, migrated to New York through the Underground Railroad during the 1800s and never returned to Charleston.

Cyrus Frazier (1852–1926) and his wife Rosa Brown Frazier (1852) had one son, Sandy Sr. (1880). After the death of Rosa, Cyrus married Rena W. Pinckney; they had two sons, Cyrus Jr. (1909) and Joseph (1913); stepson Johnny; and two daughters, Elizabeth (Lizzie) (1904) and Evelyn (1914). Cyrus's sister Dolly lived with him until she married Joseph Deleston.

According to many slaves and sharecroppers, Cyrus Frazier was the local doctor for James Island. His father, Benjamin, taught Cyrus the trade he brought from the homeland of Africa.

CONVERSATIONS WITH MY GRANDMOTHER, MARY CHAVIS FRAZIER, AND MY AUNT, EVA FRAZIER MCKELVEY

Sandy Frazier Sr. (1880–1939) and his wife Mary Chavis Frazier (1880–1963) had two sons, Sandy Jr. (1908) and James (1921); and six daughters, Rosa Frazier Kinlock (1903–1935), Eva (1913), Ethel (1917), Elouise (1920), Mary (1923) and Lela (1929); also living with the family were two nephews, Cyrus Jr. (1909) and Joseph (1913).

Over the years, during conversations with my grandma, Mary Chavis Frazier, she said,

> *Son da stom dat hit James Island [in 1893] waz real bad, it tear da top off Pa un Ma house, everting got wet. Pa, hogs un chickens waz wash way by water un we never find them. A piece of board from da storm hit cousin Princy [Prince] White un cousin Alfred Richardson on da legs un arms un hut them. We live close to Stono River wen the stom come.*
>
> *Cross da rod in front of dat tall battery on da Dill farm; da stom pick up Ms. Peggy [Peggy Gadsden] house, un chunk it down da field, she un hur child Lydia waz hut real bad. I don't tink hur ever got better from da hut before hur dead.*
>
> *Son, un dey in 1891, wen I waz a youn gal, I went on the ferry boat wid papa to see da African parade [May Day] in Charleston. A fight started un a lot of black peoples waz fighten; some got lock up by da police.*

According to Frank Deleston, he also witnessed the incident with his father, Joseph Deleston Sr.

In a conversation I had with Grandma in 1952, she said to me,

> *Son wen I waz ten years old, da waz a loud eart quake, a lot of rumbling un noise. Pa and Ma geter up all da chillin, my bubber un sisters, all of we waz under da big oak tree dat night, da people next door come to we house. All dey people hold hand un sings them old colored song un prays, all dat night un da next dey; we live close by da Stono Creek duin da stom and eart quake.*

Grandpa was a farmer and an elder in St. James Presbyterian Church. I remember him trying to teach me how to beat his drum many times on his porch before he died.

Eva Frazier McKelvey (1911) and her husband Andeas McKelvey (1911–1957) had one son, Edward. In talking with Aunt Eva over the years as she reflected back over her life, she said,

> *Son, I am the third child of your grandma and grandpa. When I was between four and five years old, I remember men and women knocking at our door day and night. They were complaining about being sick and asking for Doctor Cyrus, my grandpa Cyrus Frazier. Mama would tell the people that Grandpa Cyrus lived in the house behind us.*

Eva Frazier McKelvey, author's paternal aunt. *Family photograph.*

The peoples come from all over the island including Charleston when they were sick to see Grandpa. He was the doctor for the island; my aunt Dolly was his nurse. He had medicine in bottles and jars that he boiled from the tree roots he got out of the woods. Grandpa said he was taught how to pick roots out of the woods to make medicine by his Pa. Benjamin brought the trade from Africa.

Sometimes the people spend several days and night at Grandpa house until they were heals. Sometime they paid Grandpa with vegetables; very seldom they had any money to pay him. I remember the day he died in 1923; Fielding Funeral home hearse came to the house to pick up his body. Fielding had red velvet curtains inside the hearse to prevent peoples from seeing inside. It was a sad day. Everyone in the community was crying for Grandpa. They were crying out loud that Doctor Cyrus was gone and they had no one to doctor them.

When I was six years old, all the children had to go with their parents on the farms. We live next door to Cousin Frank Deleston and his family. I grew up with two of his daughters, Omega and Emmy. The three of us with the other children would walk with our parents to Grimball Plantation farm to pick cottons and break the corn from the stocks.

Our parents would tear croakers sack and rags; tie them together around our waist. Each person young and old would pick cotton from the long rows. We would pick cotton all day putting the cotton in the bag around our waist; the bell would ring at twelve o'clock. This meant it was time for lunch.

At the end of the day, each family member would empty their cotton in two large bundles, and tie the ends together with a special mark. The people would carry the cotton to the large shed next to the Stono River. The next day we would open the bundle, pick and separate dry leaves and stems from the cottons. The foreman would weight the cottons on a scale and pay two cents a pound for the first picking and three cents for the second picking. The Dills paid one cent a pound for picking cotton.

Mama and Papa had a small farm behind our house where they grow vegetables: rice, corn, okra, tomatoes, peanut, cabbages, collard greens, peas and potatoes. Papa had a red horse name George. He uses George to plow the fields and pull the wagon to haul the vegetables to the big boat at the dock. We would walk behind the wagon to the dock at Seabrook Landing at the end of Secessionville Road. At the landing, Papa would load the vegetable on the boat, unhitch the horse and tie him up until we get back.

Your daddy and me would ride the boat to town with Mama. When the boat reached town Mama and the other women would load they vegetables on a two-wheel pushcart. We would push the cart through the city of Charleston going from door to door selling the vegetables. When Mama and the other women finish selling their vegetables, they would leave the pushcart tied up close to one of the houses near the dock with permission from the owner.

Son, I remember one Saturday evening after Mama and the other women finish selling their vegetables, coming home on the ferry boat; one of the women was upset. She had ask a white woman at a house on Spring Street for a drink of water. The women called a policeman walking the street. She said the policeman told her, "Annie you better moves your black behind up the street before I lock you up." She was really hurt by the policemen remark. Mama and the other women told her not to cry or worry about it. God would take care of them.

I remember many times leaving Charleston riding the big boat back to James Island. The boat was full with people. Your daddy and me had to ride on top of the boat, laying flat on our stomach until it reaches the dock on James Island. During the time the roads was nothing but a trail. Grimball Road, King Hi-way, Stono Road and the other road on the island was narrow. We called them trail. The horse walked down the center of the trail pulling the wagon. We would walk in the center of the trail behind the wagon. During Labor Day, every year in September, the men that was a member of Sol Legare Lodge and King Solomon Lodge Hall would march in the parade; we called it African holiday. The men from King Solomon Lodge wear white suit, white shirt, white cap and red suspender button to they pants. The men from Sol Legare Lodge wear dark pants, white shirt, white cap or hat. The parade would start at Spring Street, to Broad Street, to King Street then ended on Spring Street near the Ashley River Bridge.

Papa and his first cousin Joe Deleston beat the two drum, while Cousin Louis Gladden beat the big bass, with another man playing the flute from King Solomon Lodge. By the time they were finished with the parade, they were wet with sweat from the hot sun. Papa's big red suspenders had turns his white shirt red in spots. When Papa got home, we could smell the moonshine whisky he been drinking on his breath.

It was a tradition of the different Lodge Hall on James Island, to beat the drum and march in funeral processional to the cemetery when a member from the lodge died. Papa, Cousin Joe Deleston and Cousin Louis Gladden would beat the drum for members of King Solomon Lodge on Stono Road [Riverland Drive]. During the holiday, they would beat the drum and play the flute and harmonica at the Lodge Hall for us to dance during the 1920s through 1930s. This was the only type of entertainment we had. We used to swing dance and shag, the same dance the white people now call "beach music," we did back in the 1920s and 1930s, in the lodge halls on James Island.

After my interview with my aunt, Eva McKelvey, I was amazed to pick up the Charleston *Post & Courier* on Thursday morning, March 6, 2003, and read with interest the headline. It stated, "The Civil Rights Movement in South Carolina Conference Scheduled at the Citadel." To my surprise just below the schedule dates was a group picture taken Labor Day, September 6, 1938, of the men from Sol Legare Lodge Hall marching in the parade.

CONVERSATIONS WITH MY AUNT, ETHEL FRAZIER CAMPBELL

Ethel Frazier Campbell (1916) and her husband Herbert Campbell (1911) had five sons, Thomas Smalls (1936), Herbert Jr., Wesley, Herman and Samuel; and three daughters, Ethel Lee, Grace and Myra.

Sol Legare Marching Band. *Courtesy of* Post & Courier.

Ethel Frazier Campbell,
author's paternal aunt. *Family
photograph.*

Aunt Ethel, over the years, told me,

Eugene, when I was six years old, the St. James Mission School had just reopened it doors in 1923, by Reverend and Mrs. Marion A. Sanders. I was in the very first class of the school along with my classmates, Ethel Richardson Turner and Mary Seabrook Goss. When the school season ended, and at the end of each school day, everyone had to work including me, even though I was only six years old. I went with Mama and my sister Eva on the Grimball, Dill, Seabrook, Clark and the Rivers Plantations to harvest vegetables.

We planted and picked cotton, corn, string beans, cucumbers, eggplant and squash. We also planted and dug white and sweet potatoes. Eugene, late in the evening, after we got home from the farm, Mama and Papa had a small seven-acre farm behind our house. We still had to work on our farm and clean around the vegetable plants with hoes and rakes while your daddy plowed the field with the horse. Papa had a red horse named George and a wagon to haul the vegetables.

When I reached the age of thirteen, your daddy married your mother. He was living with his in-laws on Turkey Pen on the Dill Plantation. While your daddy, his wife, his father and mother-in-law were all working on the Dill Farm, my mama told me I had to babysit your oldest sister, Mary Leise, while they worked. Early in the morning before sunrise, I left Grimball and walked the three miles, taking the shortcut across Cousin Paul Chisolm and Ms. Lilly Todd's properties to Riverland Drive through open fields, dense wooded areas and then wade through water across the canal that runs through the Dill Plantation. During high tide, I would tie my dress to my waist to keep it from getting wet and hold on to a rope that ran across the canal, which was tied to a bush on each side to keep us from drowning when the tide was high.

On Sunday morning when it was time for Sunday school and church, we knew, because the bell in the church steeple began ringing. Mr. James [Jim] Richardson, he was married to mama's sister; he would ring the bell until he noticed people coming to church. The people did not have clocks; they would get up in the morning when the roosters began crowing. This would tell them day was about to break.

Eugene those were some very, very hard times on James Island for black people during the 1900s. I really thank God for the black men that had the vision and the courage to lead us through those difficult years. Two brothers stand out in my mind. They got together and decided to call a community meeting of all the black people on James Island.

The topic of the meeting was how to help each other improve their lives. Richard [Dick] Singelton of Grimball, and his brother Edward [Eddie] Singelton of Sol Legare, opened the Bible and read to the people how King Solomon took care of the people during biblical times and the sacrifices the people made.

After listening, the people agreed to build a lodge hall and those who had money pooled together. Some of the men were carpenters, brick masons and blacksmiths. Most were farm workers. All pitched in together and built the lodge hall and named it King Solomon Lodge. Richard Dick Singelton was elected its first president. Although it was not chartered, it was formed on the same principle as the "Prince Hall Lodge Masonic Organization," which you and Edward belong to.

The hall is still on Riverland Drive to this day. The members held meetings to teach and invest the members with the secret password and the ritual of the lodge in order to enter. The lodge hall was a two-story building that had several kerosene oil lamps placed around the wall upstairs and downstairs to see by at night. They formed a sick committee and when someone in the community was sick, two members would visit that family and attend to their need. This might require someone to sit with the patient while the husband or wife worked. It might also include sitting with the sick and fanning them with pieces of card paper during the hot summer months and bathing and caring for them until they got better or died. In those days, we used kerosene lamps to see at night. There was no electricity in the black community.

A committee also assisted those in need of help in repairing their home. They even helped build each other's homes. It was not unusual for neighbors to send their children to each other's house to borrow a cup of sugar, flour, salt, grits, rice or coffee when their supply ran out. This was a common practice during the 1900s throughout the 1950s.

If they needed to cook soup, many parents would send their children to each other's farms to get collard greens, tomatoes or okra out of the fields. The men built a small mill behind the lodge hall. The members would bring their yellow and white corn to grind into grits and flour; and batter the rice from their husk. Some families in the community raised chickens, some hogs, goats and still others raised cows. Whenever they needed meat, one of the members would have an animal killed and send meat to the people in need.

The lodge hall was used to hold pray meetings on Tuesday and Thursday night. The members purchased two drums, a bass drum and a flute. My papa beat one of the drums. Joe Deleston, Papa's first cousin, beat the second drum and Cousin Louis Gladden beat the big bass drum. I don't recall who played the flute.

When a member of the lodge dies, a family member would report the death to the secretary who would notify the drummers. They would beat the drum until everyone in the community was notified. Boys riding horses and mules came from all over the island to find out who died. That was the way news traveled. There were no telephones during this time.

Eugene, when someone in the community died, the coffin was placed in a wagon. As the horse pulled the wagon to the cemetery, the women would be dressed in black with veils covering their faces. They walked behind the wagon as the men beat the drum all the way to the cemetery.

Shortly after the men built King Solomon Lodge, every community built their own lodge hall under the same concept founded by the members of King Solomon Lodge. The lodges were built on Central Park Road, Cut Bridge section, the Fort Johnson Road section and one in the Sol Legare community.

When I was old enough, I wanted to leave home and be on my own, but Papa refused to let the girls leave home before getting married. Papa died in 1939. I moved to the city of Charleston on Vanderhorst Street in 1940. I met my husband Herbert Campbell in 1941, and we got married that same year.

I lived on Vanderhorst Street in Charleston for several years. In 1942, my husband was drafted into the army for four years. I went in the nursing field. After my husband was discharged from the army, he went to trade school and became a brick mason and a carpenter. In 1943, my husband built this house on Burger Street in Ashleyville.

We lived next door to Ms. Lizzie Robinson. I used to sit on her porch for hours listening as she talked about slavery. She said her mother walked to Charleston barefoot. Based on what she told me, I think her mother was with the group of slaves that your great-grandpa Jake Smalls was with when they walked from South Santee to Charleston.

Ethel Frazier Campbell would become an elder in St. James Presbyterian Church and hold various positions in the church. She is a very articulate person who possesses vast amounts of information concerning the history of James Island.

CONVERSATIONS WITH MY PARENTS, SANDY FRAZIER JR. AND VIOLA SMALLS FRAZIER

Sandy Frazier Jr. (1908–1969) and his wife Viola Smalls Frazier (1908–1975) had three sons, Sandy Jr., Eugene and Jimmie; and eleven daughters, Lydia, Mary Leas, Janie Frazier Cromwell, Florence Frazier Richardson, Eva Frazier Seabrook, Ursalee, Julia Ann, Sylvia Frazier Blake, Lillie Mae Frazier Riley, Rosa Lee Frazier Fergerson and Jacqueline Frazier Hill. All the houses on the Frazier property were at one time approximately twenty-five yards behind each other.

My father told me over the years,

Son, your mother and me got married in 1926. I moved in with my father-in-law, Dan Smalls, in Turkey Pen for the first three years of our marriage. Your granduncle, Cesar Smalls, and me built this house. We started with three rooms and add rooms on to the house when I was able to. We used lumbers that float in the marshes out of the rivers; lumber I gather from the white farmer after they tore down old sheds and built new ones. The majority of people on the island were black and poor. We had to use the chimmy fireplace to cook the food and heat the house.

I stop school after Papa died to help support the family. I had to help Mama with the farm, plowing and working the land, planting and gathering vegetables to sell. In 1920, I went to work for Nungezer Farm in Fort Johnson on James Island. Ten hours a day I work on the farm, plowing with the mule, and digging drainage ditches through the fields. Late in the evening, "Bim" [Henry Galliard], one of the truck drivers, a friend, he would drive me to the Seaboard Railroad Station.

The railroad station was in the Windmere section of Charleston. People used to call the place the "Main." I unloaded trucks and stacks boxes of tomatoes, cucumber, squash and string beans into railroad car box until midnight. At the end of every season, each year George Nungezer would promise me a bonus, but he never would pay me. Son, that dog-gone man was not a fair and godly man.

Sandy Frazier Jr., author's father. *Family photograph.*

Viola Smalls Frazier, author's mother. *Family photograph.*

When I started working for Nungezer, he paid me $1.50 a week; when I quit working for him, he was paying me $40 a week. In 1948 after the death of his son little George Jr., I began doing landscape work in the Crescent, and all over the West Ashley area. Nungezer asked me if I would take care of the landscape work at his house, and the Nativity Catholic Church on Savannah Highway. Son, it was the first time I ever see him humble. I did take care of the landscape work at his home, and the church until the late 1960s.

When my father talked about how he was treated by George Nungezer, I could see the tears swell up in his eyes. He would pretend something got into his eyes. He would rub it to keep me from seeing the hurt he was experiencing. During the period when he worked on the Nungezer farms, we hardly ever saw him until the weekend because of the long hours he worked.

My father was an extremely sentimental person when it came to family. He really demonstrated his love for his family not physically, but in ways in which he was gifted, such as his ability to landscape. Each time my mother had a daughter, he would plant a rose bush for each one demonstrating to them his love and devotion to each and every one of them.

Son, in order to make ends meet, after I got home from work, I still work on our farm into the night plowing the field and do whatever it took to feed you all. Raymond Grimball did offer to sell me the property that he sold to Richard Small, next door, where he builds the Little Rock Golf Course, but I just didn't have the money.

My father would become an elder in St. James Presbyterian Church before he died. However, it was a tradition that my father, as well as others, looked to the older men such as Frank Deleston, Abraham Brown, Paul Chisolm and others for leadership, especially in cases of the death of their fathers. They believed strongly in the philosophy that it takes a village to raise a child, and they would practice this throughout their lives in the community.

My mother, Viola Smalls Frazier, over the years told me,

Son never forgets where you come from, or the advice older people give you. When I was a little girl, six years old, my sister Child "Etta Urie" and me had to work on the Dill farms picking cotton, potatoes and string beans. I went to Cut Bridge School at the corner of Stono Road and Camp Road. The school was sitting in the marsh. I went to school until I finish sixth grade; Child and me had to drop out of school and start working on the farm full time in order for our Pa and Ma to stay on the plantation.

During school season, I would walk my only brother James and a cousin, Harry Urie, to school. We lived about two miles away from the school. At the end of the school day, I would pick them up and walk them back to the cotton field to Ma. The field was in the same place where the airport was built on Riverland Drive, next to King Solomon Lodge Hall, close to the tall battery.

Ma would tie a string to a crocker sack and tie the sack around our waist. The sack holds about ten pound of cotton when it was full. After it was full, we empty them into the bundle that mama had at the end of the field. Mr. King paid one cent a pound for the first picking, and two cent for the second picking. Son we really had many hard years, but we made the best through God and prayer, so you all could have a better life than we had.

Your daddy and me got married in 1926. We lives with Ma and Pa in Turkey Pen until Uncle Cesar and your daddy was able to build this house. Son, we had a hand pump that pump well water out of the ground in Turkey Pen, and here on Grimball, but you already know that. Men from the health department use to come around and check the water to see if it was safe to drink.

The only thing we had in them days was outhouses. The health department told us we had to make sure it was far enough away from the well so it would not contaminate the water. Some of the people wells had to be condemned because they found bacteria in them; and the water had to be boiled before they could drink it.

When you were about four years old, I use to take you with me to Turkey Pen to Pa and Ma house. A lot of time I would sleep overnight. Pa used to take you walking with him everywhere he went. My first son Sandy Jr. died when he was a baby.

Pa was proud of you and said, one day you going to make something good out your life. Pa never did learn to read or write, but he knew how to sing them old Negro songs. You should remember how he used to sing to you, especially that song "Go down Moses Way down in Egypt Land," when he was working in the fields and take you walking with him.

Before going to bed at night each family member would pump a three-foot tin tub of water and then heat the water in the chimney fireplace and bathe in front of the fire at night. The fire in the chimney had to be put out before the last person goes to bed.

My Grandpa Daniel was living in a barn next door to my Aunt Etta Urie's house in Turkey Pen. During the 1940s, my mother said it was too cold for Grandpa to live in a barn during the winter months. My mother and father brought Grandpa home on Grimball to live with us; he was over eighty years old at the time. He stayed with us for about two months, became depressed and fretting; he was accustomed to the wooded areas where he would browse around in the wildness in Turkey Pen during the slavery and the farming era.

Grandpa rode in an automobile once when my Uncle James Smalls drove him back to Turkey Pen. Grandpa died in 1954. He was 101 years old. I was saddened to hear of his death. We were very close and had many conversations concerning slavery.

During the 1930s and 1940s, kerosene oil stoves made entirely of tin and a few pieces of metal weighing about twenty pounds were used primarily in the black community to heat the home. They were known as trash burners. I recall several people lost their homes because of this thin oil-burning stove. Once the stove overheated, there was no way to contain it. The house caught on fire and would burn to the ground because there was no water to put the fire out.

In our yard between the two houses were three huge oak trees. They appeared to be hundreds of years old. In fact, one of those trees still stands today in the yard on the same property where two of my aunts, Eva Frazier McKelvey and Elouise

Frazier, and my sister Julia A. Frazier still live. The tree appears to be as old as the historical Angel Oak tree on Johns Island. There were times when I looked up and gazed at that huge oak tree; it brings back mixed memories of those hard and tumultuous years in our lives.

Raymond Grimball, one of the plantation owners, came by our house to talk with my father on many occasions during the 1930s, 1940s and up to the 1950s, before I enlisted in the army; he would ride his saddle horse on Grimball Road by our house smoking his long Cuban cigar.

He would have a pack of hunting bird dogs following him. Sometimes he would take a handful of pennies out of his pocket and throw them, scattering them to the ground, and watch the children scramble for them. I never did think that was a nice thing to do to children. I never did run after his pennies.

Benjamin Frazier (1871–1943) and his wife Eliza White (1882–1944) had seven sons, Christopher, Hezekiah, Henry, Samuel, Elijah, James and William; and three daughters, Lucile, Sylvia and Hattie. Benjamin was a farmer.

Cyrus Frazier Jr. (1909) and his wife Diana McKelvey (1915) had two sons, Cyrus III and Nathan; and one daughter, Hazel. Cyrus was a farmer and was employed at the Charleston *Post & Courier*. He worked there until he retired. Cyrus was a member and an elder in the St. James Presbyterian Church on James Island. He was one of the original fifty-six men who helped to organize the Sons of Elijah Lodge #457 on James Island.

Joseph Deleston (1838) and his wife Dolly Frazier (1852) had eight daughters, Pricilla (1876), Belinda (1879), Fannie (1881), Julia (1883), Marie (1887), Annie (1889), Livinia (1891) and Rosa (1897); two sons, Frank (1875) and Joseph (Joe) (1884); and a granddaughter, Emma Brown. Dolly Frazier Deleston was the nurse and midwife for the community.

Frank Deleston (1875–1956) and his wife Annie Cromwell (1878–1948) had four sons, Samuel (1900), Cyrus (1899), Joseph Sr. (1912) and Josiah; and two daughters, Omega and Emmy.

Cousin Frank, as he was affectionately called, was a farmer. He was an elder in St. James Presbyterian Church and clerk of the session. He had a mule, wagon, plows and a cultivator, as did my father and the rest of the other farmers. He planted tomatoes, string beans, okra, squash, corn, watermelon and lima beans, among other vegetables. His wife, Cousin Annie, as she was called, had several fig trees and strawberry plants in her yard that Cousin Frank would sell on the market.

I recall during the 1930s and 1940s, my father and I would walk next door to Cousin Frank's house where everyone would gather around the battery-powered radio to listen to the news concerning World War II and heavyweight champion Joe Louis' fights. A battery-powered radio with a wire antenna on the roof of a house was a luxury for most blacks on the island during that time. Cousin Frank was among the first in our section of Grimball Road to own a battery radio.

During our youth, Cousin Frank's yard was the hangout for the boys in the community, especially during our elementary school years. His grandsons, Leon and Leroy, had a pair of boxing gloves. Every time there was a disagreement or one of the boys got angry, Cousin Frank would make us put on the boxing gloves and fight it out in a makeshift boxing ring until the anger subsided.

Most of the farmers took their vegetables to the county market in downtown Charleston every Tuesday, Thursday and Saturday to sell their vegetables. The day before going to the market all the children in the community had to help the farmers that needed help with shelling their butter beans, picking okra, tomatoes, strings beans or cucumbers and pulling peanuts. The going price to shell a quart of butter beans was three to five cents, depending on which family you were shelling for.

While we worked, men such as Prince Frazier, son of Benjamin Frazier, and Joseph Deleston, son of Frank Deleston, would tell us stories that they swore were the truth. They said that during the Civil War, the slave master would take one of his slaves into the woods to hide and bury his money in case they were overrun by the Union soldiers.

After the hole was dug and the money was placed in the hole, the slave master would kill one of the slaves and dump the body into the hole so that the spirit would guard the money. On a number of occasions, several of us (Leon, Clarence, Jackie and Sam) would notice Prince and Joseph going into these woods at night with a shovel and several feet of pipes. The pipe was the same size that plumbers used to drive into the earth to pump well water.

We would learn later that they were attempting to drive the pipe into the earth to knock a hole into the money pot. This would enable them to retrieve the money that the slave master had allegedly buried during the war. During the years we would notice several places in the woods where men had dug in search of the buried money. I was skeptical of believing this kind of myth, but could not totally dismiss it as being untrue. As a matter of fact, information from sources on the island tended to support the issue rather than disprove it.

Joe Smalls (1882) and his wife Julia Deleston (1889) had one daughter, Elsie; and grandson Alvin Washington, "Big Jimmy" (1929). Cousin Julia was a quiet women; she would sit in her rocking chair in front of her fireplace smoking her pipe and telling the children stories about her life and growing up with her brother and sister.

Her husband, Joe Smalls, died when I was very young; cousin Julia said,

Son my sisters un me waz six yea old wen we start pickin cuttin from one plantation to da oter, most we waz pay two cent a pound to pick cutting, boy yu no it tuk a long time to pick a pound of cuttin duin them time. We wok on da farms try to make end meet. I guess da Lord been wid all of we un let we live cause some dey I tink we wid not make it.

Livinia Deleston Smalls (1885–1961) and her husband Ebel (1880–1930) had one daughter, Mariah (1916–1943); and a son, Able (1924–1945). Most of the people in the community called her Cousin Mamie. I remember that day in 1943, as if it was yesterday, when Adam Davis brought Cousin Mamie and her daughter Mariah home from the doctor. He and Cousin Mamie attempted to assist Mariah out of the car and got no response and discovered Mariah had died on the way home in Adam's car.

It would be a year later that her brother, Able, was accidentally killed by a car while lying down on the ground in the yard at the intersection of Grimball Road and Riverland Drive across from Charles Whaley's house. Most of the people in the community gathered at Cousin Mamie's house to comfort the family each time. This was an accepted practice and tradition in the community to gave moral and spiritual support.

After the death of Ebel, Livinia married Louis Gladden (1878). They had two daughters, Margaret and Christina Gladden; and one son, Wallace. They also raised stepsons Abram Smalls and Sander Smalls, and Beatrice and Dolly Gibbs, Cousin Mamie's granddaughters.

Ms. Gladden and her husband Louis also had a small farm. Every Tuesday, Thursday and Saturday she would take her vegetables to the city of Charleston. They would be loaded in the two-wheel pushcart by her grandson, Clarence Gibbs, to sell in the street just as my grandma and the rest of the farmers' wives did.

Before joining the church, the young people were required to attend pray meeting every Tuesday, Thursday and Sunday night. In our community, the meeting was held at Livinia and Louis Gladden's house when it was not held in the Lodge Hall. In addition, we had to go out in the wilderness (somewhere in a wooded or private area) to pray and seek dreams that would guide the elder in telling us what church we would join and who would be our leader.

Fredrick Champagne (1899–1932) and his wife Emily Deleston (1900–1968) had three daughters, Rebecca (1924), Priscilla (1919) and Mildred; and four sons, Paul (1922), Sires (1922), Earl and Luther. Paul and Sires were twins. Emily also raised granddaughter Percile. Emily's husband Fredrick died in an accident while working on a road project that caved in on him on James Island in 1932.

In every community there was a special person to whom everyone seemed to become more attached to than others. In our community, that person in my opinion was Emily Champagne. People in the community affectionately called her Cousin Bloomy. She was a small petite woman about five feet two and weighed 115 pounds. I would sit at home when she would visit and just listen as she talked and gave advice.

She had the type of voice that made you just want to listen to her. I have heard stories of young boys who became infatuated with older women. I guess this was true concerning my feelings toward Cousin Bloomy. No matter what kind of problem someone might have in the community, after listening to her talking, that person would leave feeling that everything would get better. She seemed to possess the special qualities of a peacemaker in the community.

I recall that she would visit our house on numerous occasions talking with my mother and father. I would sit there for hours listening as she talked about the problems in the community and what needed to be done. She and my mother exchanged biscuits and cornbread many times over the years. I would accompany my mother as she visited Cousin Bloomy's house not far from our house, a place that people in the community called "On the Hill."

Joseph Deleston Sr. (1912–1968) and his wife Emily (Cord) (1912) had one son, Joseph Jr.; and one daughter, Marie. After the death of Emily, Joseph married Elizabeth Seabrook (1903). They had one son, Zenith. The people in the community

Emily Deleston. *Family photograph.*

called Joseph "St. June." He carried on the tradition of his uncle Joe Deleston of beating the drum, as did my uncle Joe Frazier, at the different lodge halls and at funerals in the community until their death. When they died, the tradition of beating the drums slowly faded away.

My mother and Emily grew up, played and went to school together; Emily was her best friend. They got married close together and worked on the farms together. She said when Emily died she grieved for a long time. Her husband, St. June, and my father were also friends and cousins. When I was a young boy, St. June was the barber in the community. He would cut the hair of both the younger males and adult males.

Joseph Deleston Jr. and his wife Ruth had three sons, Reinhardt, Antonio Frank and Jerome Lelise. Like many of the young boys in the community, Joseph Jr. worked on his grandfather Frank Deleston's farm while he attended St. James Parochial School. Following his graduation from Burke High School, he was drafted in the U.S. Army. Upon his discharge, Joseph worked at the Charleston Naval Shipyard until his retirement. Joseph followed in his father's footsteps by becoming a self-made barber, cutting the hair of the men and boys in the community and beating the drums during many of the events.

Paul Chisolm (1877–1954) and his wife Celia (1878–1946) had three sons, Benjamin (1917), Jessie (1918) and John; four daughters, Martha (1915), Ethel (1906), Rosa (1905) and Sue (1907); grandsons Paul (1922) and John (1926); and granddaughters Anna Bell (1921), Naomi (1923) and Victoria (1924). Also living with the family were Viola Richardson (1919), Celia Richardson (1925), Leroy Gilliard (1929) and an adopted son, Edward Freeman (1915).

Paul Chisolm was a farmer; he also owned three jersey cows and supplied the community with milk. Whenever my family needed milk, my mother would send me

Livinia Chisolm standing in her front yard. *Family photograph.*

Fred Doug Chisolm. *Family photograph.*

with an empty quart jar with five cents for a quart of milk. Paul and his wife Celia were nice quiet people. If the people in the community did not have money to pay, they would still get milk. No one was denied milk because of a lack of money.

Paul also planted sweet potatoes and watermelon. At night I, along with several of the boys in the community, would dig the potatoes out of the ground, build a small fire in the wooded areas next to Cousin Frank's house and roast potatoes to eat. Other nights, we would pick watermelon out of the field and eat them in the woods. We did this until we were caught. Our parents dealt with the problem with a leather strap. Needless to say, we never tried that again.

I remember when Mrs. Celia Chisolm died in 1946; the family had Fielding Funeral Home bring the body to the house. It stayed at the house for two days until the time of her burial. During the two days the young children in the community visited the house to view the body. From the 1920s until the late 1940s this was the tradition of some blacks in the community. They would sometimes have the body placed in the Lodge Hall in the community until the time of burial. Paul and Celia's son, Benjamin, is the father of my wife, Francis. He would become an important and much loved member of my family.

John Chisolm (1844–1936) and his wife Rosa (1846) had four sons, Daniel (1868), Ben (1880), John (1882) and James (1886); and five daughters, Lydia (1865), Clara (1877), Maggie (1884), Rose (1888) and Ellen (1892).

Fortune Chisolm (1864) and his wife Livinia (1877–1944) had five sons, George (1896), Ossie (1908), Ben (1911), Fred (1914) and Henry (1919); and four daughters, Julia (1911), Mattie (1920), Agnes (1922) and Elizabeth (1923). Also living with the family were nieces Margaret (1923) and Rena (1925) and nephew Samuel (1920). All were listed as mulatto with the exception of Fortune and Samuel.

Fred (Doug) Chisolm (1914–2002) and his wife Lillie Mae (1917–1991) had four sons, Fred Jr., Leon, Arthur Lee and Arnold; and three daughters, Vivian, Lucile and Audrey.

My father and Doug grew up in the same community and had many conversations over the years on virtually every subject from the Bible to fishing to farming. Doug served in the United States Navy during World War II. After he returned home, he worked at the Charleston Naval Shipyard until he retired after thirty-four years of service. Doug was a member of the First Baptist Church. He served as deacon and subsequently became chairman of the board for several years. He was very influential in the policies and general operation of the church.

Following his retirement, Doug became increasingly involved in his hobbies of fishing and working in his garden. In 1968, Doug's third oldest son, Arthur Lee, was killed during the Vietnam War. I was a Charleston County police officer at the time and provided escort service for his funeral.

I visited Doug many times over the years and had numerous conversations with him and his son, Fred Jr. I attended Burke High School with his daughters, Lucile and Vivian. During his sickness in 2002, he never complained. He was strong and talked about the Bible up to the time of his death. He was considered one of the pillars of the community.

I remember Samuel Chisolm; people in the community called him "Sammy." He spent several years in New York before returning home to James Island. When I was six years old, I would accompany my father on his visits to Chisolm Lane on many occasions. I would sit at Sammy's house while he and my father would discuss and debate the Bible.

Mr. Sammy was a fisherman and did some farming. Although many men in the community did some fishing, including my father, Chisolm Lane was the supplier of fish for the Grimball Road Community during those turbulent years. My father would also visit Ms. Livinia's house, where he and Mattie would engage in conversations.

George Chisolm (1896) and his wife Julia (1903) had one daughter, Wilimenia. According to records, George Chisolm was a World War I veteran. He operated a small grocery store in front of the Chisolm property on Grimball Road. During that era it was the only store in the community for several miles. According to several people that lived on Grimball Road, after George became sick, his brother Ossie operated the small store for a time. People called him by his nickname, "Mat Chile." Both George and Ossie are listed as mulattos.

Many of the men and women I talked with over the years said that Ossie Chisolm was sort of a Casanova in the community and that several women were attracted to him. He had at least two children with women in the community.

Ben Chisolm (1911) and his wife Maudestine had seven sons, Benjamin, Jonathan, Marion, Urie B., Nathaniel, Alexander and Henry; and two daughters, Virginia (Kitty) and Vontell (Dottie). Their son Jonathan and I served in the United States Army together as training recruits at Fort Jackson in South Carolina during the late 1950s.

John Davis (1845) was a widower. He had two sons, Fredrick (1870) and Henry (1877); and one daughter, Victoria (1893). After the death of her father, Victoria lived with her brother Fredrick until she married Mosey Wilder of the Sol Legare Plantation.

Fredrick Davis (1870) and his wife Rachel (1872–1944) had eight sons, William (Bill) (1891–1966), John (1893–1985), Christopher (1895), Hezekiah (1899), Rufus (1910), Fredrick Jr., Birmain (1912) and Adam (1914); and a granddaughter, Earline. They lived in a big two-story yellow house approximately one thousand yards from Grimball Road on a hill adjacent to the Carolina Sky Way Airport.

Adam Davis was a teacher at the St. James Parochial School for a time while I was a student there until he left Charleston in the early 1940s for one of the Northern states.

Birmain Davis was one of the few black men on James Island who owned a car during the early years. The black people depended on his family for transportation to and from Charleston. One of Fredrick's grandsons, Stanley Davis, still lives in the same house as of this writing.

D.R. Hill (1874) and his wife Martha (1882) had one daughter, Edith (1915); all were listed as mulattos. According to my father, Sandy Frazier, Mr. Hill was the principal of Society Corner School on Secessionville Road during the time he attended school.

Prince Smalls (1835–1920) and his wife Miley (1838) had four sons, Abraham (1880), Fredrick (1882), Stalling (1886) and Prince (1888); and one daughter, Rosalind (1894).

William Seabrook (1876) and his wife Isabella (1877) had one daughter, Elizabeth (Laurie) Seabrook Deleston (1903); one son, Dan Brown; and a granddaughter, Annie Deleston (1916). Mr. Seabrook was also a farmer.

Richard Cromwell (1853) and his wife Phoebe (1854) had two sons, Richard (1884) and Christopher (1897); and four daughters, Kathy (1882), Molly (1886) Laura (1888) and Emma (1893).

Richard Cromwell (1884) and his wife Wilhmenia (1890) had five sons, William, Irvin, Samuel, Oliver and Christopher; and three daughters, Ruth, Melvina and Genevise. Richard Cromwell and his daughter, Genevise, according to people in the community, were first-class carpenters and blueprint readers.

Daniel Chisolm (1868) and his wife Rebecca Kinlock (1873) had two sons, Thomas and Charles; and twelve grandchildren, as follows: Harold (1923), Arthur (1914), Eliza, Julia, Elouise, Esther, Jane Smalls (1915), Anna Smalls (1918), Bernice Smalls (1920), Helen Smalls (1926), Wilimenia Cromwell (1926) and William Harper (1926).

I remember Mrs. Rebecca. Everyone in the community called her "Cun Becker." She was one of the many women, along with my grandma and aunts, on the island who would take their vegetables to Charleston on Saturdays. Her grandson, Benjamin Smith, would push her cart through the streets for her just as the other young boys did for their grandmothers.

Harry Smith (1910) and his wife Anna (1908) had three sons, Harry Jr., Benjamin and Herman; and five daughters, Harrisena, Rebecca "Mary," Martha "Pully," Evelina "Missy" and Rose.

I knew the Smith family personally. My family lived in the same community as the Smiths and they were family friends. Mr. Harry was known by the nickname "Boy Smith." His wife was affectionately called "Chippy." She was a close friend of my mother's. The same was true of my father and her husband. The Smith families were members of St. James Presbyterian Church. Mrs. Anna worked at the American Tobacco Company.

Cuffy Brown (1874) and his wife Clara (1877) had four sons, James (1909), Franklin (1912), McKever (1914) and Scipio (1921); and six daughters, Rebecca (1902), Melvina (1916), Evelina (1918), Margaret (1926), Daisy (1917–2005) and Earline (1908).

Abraham (Humble) Brown (1885–1975) and his wife Estelle (1906) had three sons, Joseph, Ervin and Daniel (1920); and four daughters, Fannie (1922), Ersalee (1917), Evelina (1927) and Livinia (1929). After the death of Estelle, Abraham married Essie Brown. They had five daughters, Evelyn, Cecile, Jane, Verna Lee and Mable; and one son, Kenneth. People in the community called Abraham "Cousin Humble." He was also a farmer. He was a tall man, probably six foot three; he was also an elder in St. James Presbyterian Church. I don't know for sure but I guess the people in the community gave him that nickname because he was really a quiet and a humble man.

McKever Brown (1914) and his wife Ora Lee had two sons, Gordon and McKever Jr.; and five daughters, Florence Ethel, Annie Laura, Isabelle, Patricia Ann and Vanessa. According to McKever Jr., his father also had two other children, Janie Frazier Weston and Samuel Frazier.

Henry Whaley Sr. *Family photograph.*

Gordon Brown, the eldest son, was inducted into the African American Golfer Hall of Fame on May 29, 2005, in Fort Lauderdale, Florida.

The family residing south on the dirt trail next to the Stono River was James Whaley (1822) and his wife Charlotte (1824).

Henry Whaley (1861) and his wife Peggy Singelton (1864) had three sons, Charles (1890), Elias (1894) and Enoch (1900); and seven daughters, Pauline (1888), Hermenia, Anna M. (1886), Mariah (1895), Elizabeth (1892–1966), Isabel (1896–1956) and Emma (1898).

Elias Whaley (1894–1967) and his wife Melvina Richardson (1900) had two sons, Elias Jr. (1919) and Lorenzo (1917); and five daughters, Janie (1921), Wilamena (1923), Belle (1926), Evelyn (1929) and Gracie (1930). After the death of his first wife Melvina, Elias married his second wife, Venus Goss. Elias was the foreman, handyman, driver and captain of a boat called the *Seminole* for the Grimball Plantation.

I recall that Elias was the first black person on the island to have a telephone. This telephone was a direct line that ran from the Grimball Plantation house to Elias's house. If a black person in the community had an emergency, they would run to Elias's house. He would crank up the old phone and relay the message to the Grimballs. The Grimballs would in turn notify the doctor or police.

Elias was also among the first group of black people that owned an automobile on the island. People in the community called him Papa Light and Cou-Nina. He was a member of the First Baptist Church on James Island, chairman of the Deacon Board and a class leader.

Levola Whaley. *Family photograph.*

Elias (Jake) Whaley Jr. (1919) and his wife Levola Wallace (1927) had one daughter, Sonia Whaley Simmons. Everyone in the community affectionately called Elias by his nickname, "Jake." He had this memorable quote that he greeted everyone with: "Live and let live, and live to die, and live to live again." As I was growing up, I paid little attention to these quotes of Jake but as time passed, I realized that those quotes of Jake were what his life was all about and how he lived. When I was a young boy, Jake and his brother Lorenzo worked for H.W. Halter and Son Meat Company on James Island. They supplied many people on the Grimball Plantation who were unable to afford it with meat during those trying times.

Jake and Lorenzo would share what they had with those in need; this was the custom of the people living on the plantation during this time. Jake served in the United States Army during World War II and returned home in 1945. He was discharged in 1946. Jake and Levola Wallace Whaley were married in 1946. Jake was a likable and pleasant man in the community who everyone enjoyed talking with. Many times I just enjoyed listening as he quoted verses from the Bible.

Levola Wallace Whaley grew up on the Sol Legare section of James Island. As I talked with Levola over the years she said,

> *Frazier, I never knew my mother Rebecca Wallace, she died when I was one and a half years old. I had two brothers and five sisters. I received my elementary education at the Patrick School on Sol Legare.*
>
> *After I completed middle school, they were no high schools on James Island for black students. Those students that wanted a high school education and their parents that could afford it had to attend Burke or Avery High School. It was located in the city of Charleston some seven miles away. Those of us that decided to go to high school had to find our own transportation. South Carolina did not furnish school buses for African Americans in those days.*
>
> *We had to brave the cold, the hot sun and the rain standing by Folly Road waiting for a ride to go to school, sometimes walking the seven miles. During that time, very few blacks had cars and trucks on the island. However, those who did would give us a ride to school on their way to work.*
>
> *I took courses at South Carolina State College and the University of South Carolina for my bachelor degree. As you already know, I taught at St. James Parochial School for four years. I taught for thirty-four years in the Charleston County School system. I received my master's degree in education from the Citadel Military College in Charleston, South Carolina.*

Levola received many awards while she taught in the school system. She is presently a member of the Daughters of Elijah #337 order of the Eastern Star Lodge, Charleston Alumni Chapter of Delta Sigma Theta Sorority, Inc., and an active member of St. James Presbyterian Church. Levola served as Sunday school superintendent, an elder on the Presbyterian Women's Organizations, Session Board and many more too numerous to mention. Levola was my elementary school teacher at St. James Parochial School.

Lorenzo Whaley (1916–1997) and his wife Mattie Palmer (1917) had one son, Lorenzo Jr.; and five daughters, Melvina, Kathleen, Phyllis, Olivia and Jacqueline.

Lorenzo was employed by H.W. Halter and Son Meat Company for many years. He was later employed by Emanuel-El Synagogue until he retired. I remember Lorenzo as a quiet, easygoing person who would greet you with a smile and "how you doing." Like his brother Jake, he was generous in the community. I cannot recall anyone in the community that had anything negative to say about Lorenzo.

Joseph Enoch Whaley Sr. (1900–1950) and his wife Celestine (1903–1991) had three sons, Joseph Jr. (1924), Thomas (1922) and Danny (1925). Joseph was a farmer, but I remember him doing a lot of fishing. I recall he and my father would go fishing, sometimes twice a week at night, after my father got off from work. They would go casting for fish in the Stono River in a rowboat he and my father built.

On Tuesdays and Saturdays, Enoch and my father would buy fifty pounds of ice from an iceman selling ice on the island. They would chip the ice in small pieces in a three-foot tin tub to keep the fish from spoiling. On these days they would hitch the mule to the wagon and drive through the community selling their mullet and whiting fish. If the people in the community did not have money to pay, they would still let them have the fish and pay when, and if, they could.

Most of the people on the island were poor and helped each other when the need occurred. Enoch died in 1950; his death really affected my father. I could always tell by the look in his eyes when he was hurt. They were very close friends. My father also had a hobby: he liked making casting nets. I watched him on numerous occasions knitting casting nets for men in the community. In fact, he taught my uncle James Smalls how to make casting nets.

Joseph Whaley Jr., the son of Enoch, said,

> Frazier, I would ride on the Seminole boat with my uncle Elias during the 1930s hauling vegetables. The boat would be loaded with potatoes, cabbages and whatever vegetable was in season at the time. The workers sometimes worked through the night on Thursday to have the boat loaded by Friday morning. My uncle Elias would drive the boat north, on the Stono River, through Wappoo Cut Bridge along South Battery and the Cooper River to Adgers where the boat would be unloaded.
>
> There was a kitchen dining and sleeping area on the boat; some weekends, Uncle Elias would take Raymond Grimball and some of his friends to Kiawah Island to hunt. They would stay the weekend and sleep overnight on the boat. Uncle Elias would cook for the men while they were hunting until they returned home to James Island.

At the end of Cuffy Lane lived Cudjo Chavis (1813) and his wife Mary (1814). They had three sons, Paul (1841), Swinton (1846) and Thomas (1855); and three daughters, Sally Chavis Geddis, Hanna Chavis Geddis and Elizabeth. Cudjo and Mary Chavis were my great-great-grandparents. Cudjo and Mary came from Sierra Leone to this country to Eloree, in Orangeburg County, South Carolina, and then migrated to Charleston, where they became sharecroppers on the Grimball and the Dill Plantations.

Paul Chavis (1841–1925) and his wife Betsy Matthew (1850) had four daughters, Mary Chavis Frazier (1880–1960), Irene Chavis Gilliard (1895–1949), Alice Chavis McNeal (1875–1949), and Julia A. Chavis Richardson (1897); and six sons, Joseph (1882–1936), Thomas (1890), John (1878), William (1885), Joe (1885) and George (1891). Also living with the family were granddaughter Ellen (1914) and grandson Alonzo (1916).

After the death of Betsy, Paul Chavis married Rebecca Matthew Lawton, the sister of Betsy, who took care of her during her illness; there were no children. Records in the RMC office book #023 in Charleston County dated May of 1879 show that he purchased the property where he and his family lived from Lula Grimball of the Grimball Plantation.

Robert Gilliard Sr. (1893) and his wife Irene Chavis (1895–1949) had three sons, Robert Jr. (1915), Henry and John; and six daughters, Mabel (1919), Agnes (1918), Lucile, Elizabeth and Carrie. Robert and Irene were farmers. After the death of her husband, Irene continued to support her family by farming and taking her vegetables to Charleston to sell in the streets door to door, as her sister, Mary Chavis Frazier, did. She farmed the Chavis property until her death in 1949. She is buried in the Burn Church Cemetery at Folly Road and Fort Johnson Road.

John Chavis (1878) and his wife Martha (1883) had five sons, Fred (1908), John Jr. (1909), Edward (1912), Julius (1917) and Hazel (Dock) (1912); and five daughters, Eva (1913), Lavinia (1906), Amy (1911) Nomi (1914) and Rebecca (1916). After the death of John, Martha married Thomas Gourdine.

William Chavis (1885) and his wife Christina Deleston (1893) had one son, Richard (1919); and three daughters, Wilimenia Chavis Frazier (1917–2002), Catherine Chavis McFadden (1925–2001) and Julia Chavis Darden (1928–2003).

George Chavis (1891) and his wife Alberta Morgan had two sons, George Jr. and Leon; and two daughters, Elizabeth and Mildred. George had two children with his first wife, Ellen (1914) and Alonzo (1916). I recall when I was a young boy, nine years old, my grand-uncle, George Chavis, would sit on my Grandma Mary Chavis Frazier's porch. During several conversations with my father over the years he would discuss how he and his father, Paul Chavis, would walk to and from Eloree, South Carolina.

In one of those conversations, he said,

> *Boise sometimes it take we days to walks to Eloree and back to Jim Island* [James Island was also referred to as "Jim" Island by many of the black people]. *Yu know that waz my Pa's home when he fuss comes to South Carolina. Sometime we jump off the road and hide into the bush from the Ku Klux Klan's men with hood over they head ridin horses. We did not know what dey wid do so we hide until dey pass. Boise we pray, wok hard serves God and we made it this fur, God will always take care of we.*

I remember Uncle George. He was a brave strong black man who was unafraid of any man, one on one, and would not hesitate to express his opinion.

Joseph "Joe" Frazier (1913) and his wife Wilhmenia (1917–2001) had four sons, Joseph Jr., Johnny, John and James; and two daughters, Rosa Bell and Louise. In my conversations with Uncle Joe over the years, he said,

Son, me un yu papa come up in hard time. Yu grandpa dead wen we waz youn, he raised me cause my papa dead fore him. Yu papa un me had to stop tool [school] uley [early] to help support dey family.

Yu papa was older un me. I tart wok wen I waz eight yea old; pickin cuttin, cun, tater, cabbage, squash, cucumber un matos. We wok on da Grimballs', Dills', Clarks', Ellis's un Rivers' farm. Wen I waz thirteen I tart wokin on George Nungezer farms. I plow dey felds wid mules, diggin trench to dey fields to water da plants.

Wen it waz time to geter dey crop, we pack um in crate un box and take to dey railroad tatuin [station] on da Main; dat wha yu papa wid load un tack em in railroad car boxes to be shipped out. Yu papa waz a tron [strong] man un did da wok of two man. Nungezer pay we $1.50 cent a week wen I tart wokin on da farm.

Yu grandpa lun [learn] me how to beat da drum, me un yu papa uta march in dey parade wid yu grandpa, Cousin Louis Gladden un Cousin Joe Deleston. While dey beat da drum in town every September, St. June [Joseph Deleston] un me carry on dey trade [tradition]. After da deth of yu Grandpa, St June un me wid beat da drum as people marched to dey graveyard to bury dey dead. We beat em at King Solomon Lodge Hall, on holiday un lot of oter holidays.

Richard (Dick) Singelton (1883) and his wife Christina (1888) had four sons, Louis, Richard, Willis and James; and two daughters, Dorothy (1907) and Sarah Ann. The Singelton house once stood on the property that the W.G. Meggett High School and Septima Clark Academy now occupies.

Richard "Dick" Singelton later moved to the Secessionville Road community, where some of his descendants still live. He was a farmer, carpenter and also did masonry work. He and his sons were very knowledgeable and articulate people.

Mr. Singelton helped build and organize King Solomon Lodge Hall on Riverland Drive. He was instrumental in helping various other lodges on the islands organize. He was an elder in the St. James Presbyterian Church. He had two sisters, Emma and Mamie. He was considered one of the pillars in the black community.

Louis Singelton (1846) and his wife Sarah (1856) had five sons, Eddie (1881), Richard (Dick) (1883), Isaac (1886), Joe (1896) and William (1897); and four daughters, Margaret (1888), Tena (1890), Janey (1892) and Christine (1892).

Limus Smalls (1867–1944) and his wife Betsy (1870–1944) had three sons, Isaiah (1892), Roosevelt and Robert. I recall Limus had several pecan trees in his yard and would sell pecans in addition to his vegetables.

Directly behind his house was the home of his son Isaiah (1892) and his wife Mary Simmons Smalls (1896). They had three sons, Benny, Morris and Prince; and three daughters, Catharine, Betsy and Albertha. Benny and Prince moved to New York during the 1940s, making it their home.

Morris Smalls Sr. (1916–1984) and his wife Vernell Cromwell (1919) had one son, Morris Jr.; and three daughters, Berthel Smalls Ward, Elaine Smalls Able and Ruby Smalls Senior. Morris was educated at Society Corner School and became a member of the First Baptist Church on James Island. He served in the United States Navy during World War II.

Following his discharge from the navy, Morris was hired at the Charleston Naval Base Shipyard. He was the first African American to attend the training school for plumbers in Charleston. He became the first black instructor of the plumbing and pipefitting shop during the years when segregation was enforced; he worked over thirty-five years before he retired in 1980.

Morris was a congenial type person—one of those people in the community whom everyone got along with. His professional knowledge and skills helped numerous people in the community. Nicknames that were given to him by friends included Dollar Bill, Millions, Rorge and Stiney.

From the 1950s through the 1970s, Morris helped his brother Richard Smalls operate the Little Rock Golf Club. It was a combination of a six-hole golf course and a nightclub that stood next door to the Fraziers' property.

This was the only place where black men could play golf during those years, until the Charleston Municipal Golf Course was integrated. On this property now stands the Little Rock Boulevard. It is a twenty-eight-house community on Grimball Road. Upon his retirement in 1980, Morris lived in New York until his death in 1984. His family brought him home to be buried.

Daniel McNeil (1841) and his wife Moria (1841) had two daughters, Jane (1865) and Sylvia (1881); two sons, Henry (1869) and Robert (1874); and a son-in-law, Jimmie Gilliard (1878). Daniel McNeil was the son of a black woman and a white man believed to be one of the plantation owners. His wife Moria was of Indian descent and was believed to have migrated from the Pineville area.

Sarah and Daniel McNeil. *Family photograph.*

Robert McNeil (1874) and his wife Alice Chavis (1875–1949) had four daughters, Josephine McNeil Judge (1896), Emily (1898), Lizzie (1899) and Sylvia (1907). After the marriage between Robert McNeil and Alice Chavis, my grand-aunt moved from the dead end of Cuffie Lane with her husband Robert to Barnhill on Grimball Plantation and to Sol Legare Plantation.

Moses McNeil (1890) and his wife Mary (1891) had one son, Oliver (1918); three daughters, Charlotte (1922), Albertha (1924) and Mary Jane (1926); and a niece, Katie Gilliard (1913); all were living with them.

I remember Mr. Moses McNeil. He was a carpenter, built homes and repaired numerous houses on James Island. During the 1940s, I recall two rooms and the kitchen on my grandma's house were severely damaged by fire. Moses rebuilt the rooms and the chimney.

James Prioleau (1823) and his wife Rebecca (1831) had four daughters, Betty (1854), Louisa (1859), Harriett (1855) and Ellen (1869); and a son, Sancho (1855).

James Prioleau's second wife was Betsy (1835). Also residing with them were Thomas Gourdine (1872), Theodore Gourdine (1886), Walter Gourdine (1871) and Betsy Gourdine (1883).

James Prioleau came to Charleston from Orangeburg County (Pineville), where he was a young slave. Over a period of many years, James Prioleau purchased over one hundred acres of property from the Grimball Plantation. James Prioleau was indeed a man ahead of his time. He had the vision, the drive and the desire to use his physical stamina and his attitude for saving coupled with an incredible vision to secure a financial future for his family and his future descendants.

As a freedman he became a sharecropper and eventually a farmer on the property he purchased from the Grimballs. Prior to his death, he left a will dividing the land among his children. Many of his descendants, which include my children, still live on the land left by their ancestor, James Prioleau. A major portion of that land is located on Grimball Road in an area referred to as "Barnhill."

Louisa Prioleau Young, the daughter of James Prioleau, was married to Moses Young (1862). They had one son, Walter; and one daughter, Wilhelmina Prioleau Cromwell. Walter Prioleau would later marry Hettie Gadsden. They would become the grandparents of my wife, Francis Prioleau Frazier.

CONVERSATIONS WITH MARY "FEEDIE" ROPER

James Roper Sr. (1890) and his wife Mary Champagne (1888–1989) had six sons, Morris (1911), Samuel (1923), Ned (1918), James Jr. (1919), Herman (1922) and Arthur (1930); and five daughters, Janie (1920), Marguerite (1925), Naomi (1926), Bessie (1928) and Alice (1933).

Mary married James Roper in 1912 and moved with her husband from the Dill Plantation, where her parents were slaves and sharecroppers, to the Grimball Plantation, where her husband was a farmer. Mary was affectionately called "Cousin Feedie" by everyone in the community who knew her.

Louisa Prioleau Young. *Family photograph.*

She was a midwife and received her medical training at the medical health institute in Sumter, South Carolina. I recall on one occasion talking with her over the years. She said, "Son I deliver over a thousand babies here on James Island and in the city, including some white babies whose parents were poor like us and could not afford a doctor."

Cousin Feedie had an arrangement with one of the bakeries on Cannon Street in Charleston during the 1930s through the 1940s. She would collect the bread and cake that was returned from the store to the bakery and bring it all home to James Island. She would supply the entire community with the leftover bread, sweet muffins and cake. People welcomed the bread and cake. For many families, it was the only sweets they could afford.

On numerous occasions during the early 1940s, my father would give me a quarter and send me to Cousin Feedie's house riding the horse to buy bread and cake. She would fill the little sack with bread and cake and then give me the quarter back. She said, "Tell your daddy that everything okay, I know he have a lot of mouth to feed." If you knew Cousin Feedie, there was no way that you walked away without loving her; she was one of the true matriarchs of James Island.

I recall a conversation with her during the 1970s; she said, "Son, let me make you laughs. One day during the early 1900s, my sons, Ned and Morris, were outside playing in the yard. They came running inside the house screaming that there was a horse going down the road with no head. I went outside to looks; it was the first time the children had seen a car on James Island driving down Grimball Road."

She was a member of St. James Presbyterian Church for eighty-seven years and belonged to several organizations on the island. Feedie and my grandmother-in-law, Hettie Gadsden Prioleau, were close friends. Both were born and raised on the Dill Plantation. Following their marriages, both moved to the Grimball Plantation with their husbands. Both lived a long and prosperous life. Mary (Feedie) Roper died in 1989 at the age of 101.

John Prioleau (1897–1985) and his wife Mary Gilliard (1899) had three sons, James (1923), John (1933) and William (1939); and five daughters, Viola (1925), Ethel (1927), Laura (1929), Mary (1935) and Edith (1935).

John Prioleau served in the U.S. Army during World War I; he was a farmer and a member and elder of St. James Presbyterian Church. Following Elder Frank Deleston's tenure as clerk, John became the clerk of session.

Isaac Gourdine (1881) and his wife Rilla (1882) had two sons, Joe (1905) and Alfred (1909); four daughters, Lizzie (1910), Aleta (1913), Ida (1914) and Mary (1917); and two grandsons, Leonard (1928) and James (1918). Isaac is listed as mulatto.

Hen Jana Judge (1875), a widow, had two sons, Arthur Middleton (1897, and Charles Middleton (1901); and three daughters, Catharine Middleton (1906), Julia Middleton (1902) and Edith Middleton (1906). She also had three daughters-in-law, Bertha Middleton (1923), Emma Middleton (1922) and Betty Middleton (1927); and four grandsons, Arthur Middleton Jr. (1925), Ben Middleton (1925), Julian Middleton (1928) and Carl Middleton (1922).

Ben Prioleau (1910) and his wife Helen Richardson (1915) had nine daughters, Evelyn, Alice, Elizabeth, Catherine, Naomi Prioleau, Sarah Ann Prioleau, Helen Prioleau, Cecile Prioleau and Julia Prioleau; and two sons, Benjamin Prioleau and Ronny Prioleau. Helen was a member and an elder of St. James Presbyterian Church.

Helen's daughter, Alice, and I attended the St. James Parochial School together, where Alice and I developed a close personal friendship. Upon finishing middle school, I attended Burke High in Charleston, and Alice attended W.G. Meggett High school on James Island. After leaving Burke, I enlisted in the U.S. Army and Alice went to New York. We briefly lost touch with each other but remained friends over the years.

Ossie Moore (1892) and his wife Jennie (1895) had three sons, Elijah (1919), John (1921) and Reese (1923); and two daughters, Gertie L. (1925) and Lindy (1927).

Jacob Pettigrew (1889) and his wife Julia (1891) had six daughters, Isabelle, Anna, Amanda, Evelyna, Mary and Phyllis; and four sons, John, James, Josiah and Samuel.

Josiah Brown (1870) and his wife Clohie Carrie (1881–1965) had four daughters, Anethia (1905), Henrietta (1907), Leona (1918) and Dorothy (1921); and four sons, Elijah (1903), Josiah Jr. (1915), Isaac (1911) and Willis (1923).

George Thomas (1920) and his wife Dorothy Brown (1921) had one son George Jr.; and one daughter, Doris. During several conversations with Dorothy Thomas between the years 1999 and 2004, the youngest daughter of Josiah Brown said,

Frazier, we grows up on the farm like everyone else, I got married to my husband George in 1950 and moved to Charleston.

We had two children, my son George Jr. and my daughter Doris. My husband worked for the Gulf Oil Company for thirty-four years and was a good provider. He was a plumber by trade and worked for many families in the Charleston area. I was a housewife and took care of my children and proud of the way they grow up to be. I was able to graduate from C.A. Brown High School and was proud to receive my diploma.

Josiah Brown (1915) and his wife Helen had one daughter Dorothy Johnson. Josiah served in the United States Army during World War II and was wounded in action and received a purple heart and a bronze medal.

George Gilliard (1873) and his wife Laura (1873) had three sons, Robert (1893), Alexander (1893) and Charles (1897). After the death of her husband George, Laura Gilliard married Plenty Jackson of the Sol Legare Plantation. Robert Gilliard was married to my grand-aunt, Irene Chavis. He was a farmer and moved to the Chavis property at the end of Cuffy Lane off Grimball Road, where he worked on his farm until his death.

Albert Gilliard (1888) and his wife Florence (1894) had one daughter, Nellie (1911); stepdaughters Minerva Taylor (1915), Ida Lee Brown (1919), May Belle Brown (1918), Lucinda Brown (1922) and Inez Brown (1926); and stepson Sam Brown (1913).

Alexander Gilliard (1895) and his wife Elizabeth (1900) had four sons, Sam (1920), Alexander Jr. (1922), George (1925) and Joseph; and two daughters, Emma (1918) and Dorothy.

Henry Singelton (1925–2005) and his wife Evelyn Brown (1927) had seven daughters, Lucile, Gloria, Betty Ann, Mary Louise, Jeanette, Angela and Marcella; and two sons, Henry Jr. and Remus Brown.

Henry was affectionally called Dad by people in the community. He was one of the original fifty-six men who founded the Sons of Elijah Masonic Lodge on James Island. He was a member of St. James Presbyterian Church on James Island. I remember him as a humble man.

Henry Moultrie (1898) and his wife Rosa Deleston (1895) had five sons, March (1919), John (1921), Franklin (1925), Henry Jr. (1927) and William (1929); and three daughters, Lilly (1923), Patsy (1924) and Mary J. (1927).

March West (1880) and his wife Lizzie (1892) had three sons, Frank (1913), Abraham (1923) and Jeffries (1917); and daughter-in-law Catherine (1911). After the death of Lizzie, March married his second wife, Patsy.

Josiah Campbell (1895) and his wife Betsy (1898) had three daughters, Viola Campbell White, Emily Campbell and Nellie Campbell Moultrie; and four sons, Richard, Tony, Weston and Josiah. Betsy was listed as a mulatto.

John Roper Sr. (1908) and his wife Ernestine Lafayette (1912) had six sons, John H. Jr., William H., Russell, Ernest R., Kenneth E. and Bernard L.; and one daughter, Francine. Mr. Roper graduated from Avery Institute of Charleston in 1931. He met and married his wife, Ernestine Lafayette of James Island, in 1932.

John served in the United States Army during World War II. After his discharge, he taught agriculture and home skills to veterans returning from the war. I recalled

Mr. Roper teaching Sunday school at the St. James Presbyterian Church. I was one of his students. He worked at the Francis Marion Hotel for a time. He was among the first black men hired by the United States Post Office in Charleston and was considered a pioneer. I remember Mr. Roper as an articulate and very knowledgeable person in the English language.

Marion A. Sanders (1888) and his wife Ona Belle (1898) had three sons, Marion A. Jr., (1921), Leroy J. (1923) and Wilburn M. (1925); and two nieces, Edna R. Montgomery (1904) and Lilly M. Sanders (1920). Reverend Marion Sanders and his wife, Ona Belle, migrated from Charlotte, North Carolina, to accept the call as pastor of the St. James Presbyterian Church at Fort Johnson and Secessionville Road in 1923.

Isaac Richardson (1881) and his wife Liza (1891) had four daughters, Henrietta (1911), Ethel (1912), Martha (1916) and Betsy (1922); two sons, Joseph (1912) and Elias (1919); and grandson Hezekiah (1929).

Martha Richardson Gladden (1916) and her husband Bennie Gladden (1912) had one son, Ralph Richardson. I interviewed Mrs. Gladden and had numerous conversations with her over the years. She said,

> *Eugene, my family grew up poor on James Island just like the rest of the people.*
>
> *When I was young, I grew up with three sisters, and two brothers. I attended the St. James Parochial School, which ended at eighth grade. The same school you went to. As you well aware they were no high schools on James Island for blacks. Those of us who wanted a high school education and whose parents could afford it had to attend Burke Industrial, Avery or Immaculate Conception High School in Charleston.*
>
> *I chose Immaculate Conception. The problem was getting to school in the morning. Most of the time, we left home early enough to walk to school. Sometimes a black man would come by in an old truck or car and would stop and give us a ride. Mornings when it rains my daddy would load us in the back of his truck and take us to school. At the end of the school day, if it was raining too hard, my daddy would pick us up. South Carolina refused to provide school buses to transport black students during the 1920s, and up to the 1950s.*
>
> *Eugene, you know that all the roads on James Island were dirt surface. When it rained, the road was muddy and the few trucks and cars on the island got stuck. These were very difficult times for blacks, but we kept the faith in God and prevailed. After I completed my education, I married my husband Benny in 1943. I began teaching that same year at the St. James Parochial School where I graduated from.*

Mrs. Gladden was my teacher in elementary school and she had a car. I recall she would give rides to students that lived miles away on the Cut Bridge Section of the island to school. Mrs. Gladden was one of those teachers who made you feel comfortable being around her and had that motherly image about her.

She became a member of St. James Presbyterian Church during her teenage years and held several positions in the church, including elder and Sunday school teacher. She is one of those quiet soft-spoken people that you could not help but love. Mrs.

Junius Richardson. *Family photograph.*

Gladden would go the last mile to help you if she could. She retired from teaching in 1989, and still is an active member in St. James Presbyterian Church as of this writing.

CONVERSATIONS WITH ALONZO RICHARDSON REGARDING HIS FATHER, JUNIUS RICHARDSON

Junius Richardson (1899) and his wife Lillian Drayton (1903) had five daughters, Marguerite (1922), Julia Bell (1926), May, Edith and Deloris; and four sons, Eugene, Walter, Perry and Alonzo.

During conversations with Alonzo Richardson, son of Junius, he said,

> *Frazier, my daddy worked for the Massenburg family that owned and operated a shrimp company on Folly Beach during the 1920s through the 1940s. He was one of the boat captains that operated a shrimp and fish trawler in local water and in the Atlantic Ocean catching and hauling shrimp.*
>
> *He would bring the shrimp into Massenburg Dock at Folly Beach where the black people were working. They would clean and take the heads off the shrimp and fish and then pack it up to be shipped to buyers throughout Charleston County and other places.*
>
> *Daddy and Uncle Jim during the 1930s through the 1940s would meet boats coming in from Cuba loaded with whiskey in the Stono River near the Dills Plantation. He would haul the liquor to the Massenburg Dock where it would be distributed to a local dealer. Daddy said several times over the years, while hauling the liquor, he and Uncle Jim would break one bottle in at least two of the cases before reaching the dock.*
>
> *After Massenburg counted the cases, he would give daddy and Uncle Jim the cases with the broken bottle. They would go around to the local Juke Joint and sell the liquor for themselves. This old compass is the one Daddy used on the shrimp trawler when he was the boat captain. Daddy said on a foggy or black night when there was no moon, he had his compass set so he could maneuver through the river without light.*
>
> *Daddy would leave home and be gone sometimes for two weeks at a time. Unbeknown to Mama every time he returned home, he would buy lumber and store them under Grandpa's house. Mama was in shock one day when she realized he had saved enough money to pay old man Dick [Richard] Singelton to help him build the house on Battery Island where our family was born and raised. Daddy was the first black man on James Island that owned and drove a new Cadillac.*

Many of the older black men on James Island confirmed Alonzo's recollection of his father's history, including my father, Sandy Frazier.

Note the article written in the past by some authors lists Junius Richardson (1899) as a state constable. This is incorrect; it was Julius Richardson (1876) who was the state constable.

Cecil Richardson, first black engineer, standing on the Wappoo Bridge. *Family photograph.*

James (Jim) Richardson (1891) and his wife Julia Chavis (1895) had one son, Willie (1917). After the death of Julia, James married Mamie Richardson. They had one son, William Backman (1929). Jim was the custodian for the St. James Presbyterian Church.

Every Sunday morning around nine o'clock, Jim would go into the church steeple and begin ringing the bell to let the people know it was time for church. He did this chore until the 1940s. He was a small petite man who stood about five foot two—a quiet and a humble man. Julia Chavis, his first wife, was my grand-aunt.

Julius Richardson (1876) and his wife Rachial (1878) had two daughters, Olivia (1893) and Lottie. Julius was one of the black constables on James Island during the 1800s.

Frank Richardson (1880) and his wife Celia (1890) had three daughters. Catherine (1913), Sarah (1915) and Hannah (1920); three sons, Cecil (1909), Robert (1911) and Frank Jr. (1917); grandsons William and Louis; and granddaughter Bertha.

Cecil Richardson (1904) and his wife Charlotte (1907) had one daughter, Maria (1927). Cecil was the first known African American engineer that operated a drawbridge here in Charleston. He operated the Wappoo Cut Bridge for years before he retired from the South Carolina Highway Department on James Island.

Henry Richardson Sr. (1861) and his wife Mary (1885) had two daughters, Janie (1914) and Pricilla (1911); and two sons, Isaac (1910) and Henry Jr.

John Harker (1868) and his wife Betsy (1871) had three daughters, Lottie (1897), Mary (1898) and Louisa (1915); and three sons, Abraham (1890), William (1900) and Sam (1911). According to Harold Singelton, William Harker would follow the Labor Day parade in the city of Charleston annually. This would confirm why he was in the picture taken on September 6, 1938, walking behind the men of Sol Legare Lodge in the parade held in the city of Charleston.

Richard Backman (1839) and his wife Mae (1850) had one son, Primus (1862); and three daughters, Cola (1868), Sarah (1869) and Louisa (1857).

Richard Backman (1876) and his wife Jennie (1895) had three sons, Thomas (1919), Moses (1922) and Richard (1924); one daughter, Julia (1920); and granddaughter Virginia (1929).

Timothy Backman (1882) and his wife Josephine (1881) had living with them grandson Timothy (1927); stepson William Harker (1921); and stepdaughter Elizabeth Heyward (1922).

William McLeod, owner of McLeod Plantation. *Family photograph.*

THE McLEOD
PLANTATION OWNERS

WILLIAM McLEOD (1820) AND HIS wife Susan (1822) had one daughter, Margaret (1845). John McLeod (1810) had one son, William W. (1850), who was married to Hallie (1849). They had a son, Willie E. (1885). Joseph McLeod (1812) had two daughters, Wilhelmina (1838) and Martha (1840).

The McLeod Plantation stretched from the Wappoo Cut River through the marsh area where the Country Club Golf Course is now located and the slave cabins stood at Maybank Highway and Folly Road. The plantation stretched south to Harborview Road then across Folly Road, covering the area where the Piggly Wiggly shopping center now sits at Maybank Highway and Folly Road, to the Wappoo Bridge. Some of the cabins that were built for slaves during the period of slavery are still intact and are located at the corner of Maybank Highway and Folly Road.

The slave schedule from 1850 to 1860 shows that the McLeod family owned ninety-five slaves, including twenty mulattos, during these years.

SLAVES AND THEIR DESCENDANTS RESIDING ON THE McLEOD PLANTATION

Stephen Forest Sr. (1844) and his wife Harriet (1844) had two sons, Stephen Jr. (1870) and Coleman (1895).

At the outbreak of the Civil War, Brigadier General S.R. Gist of the Confederate army ordered the evacuation of James Island. He stated that each plantation owner was allowed to leave one male and a female slave behind to watch over their plantations. William McLeod entrusted his property to Stephen and Harriet Forest.

As the war progressed in 1865, the plantation was taken over by the black Massachusetts Fifty-fourth and Fifty-fifth Regiments for their headquarters and division hospital. Following the war, the Freedmen's Bureau was set up by the government on the McLeod Plantation to assist the newly freed slaves. The head of each slave family, thirty-seven to be exact, was granted land by the government.

Steve Forest (1906) and his wife Eva (1912) had two sons, James (1925) and Harry (1929); and two daughters, Livinia (1923) and Joann.

Slave house on McLeod Plantation located on Folly Road. *Family photograph.*

I recall as a young boy attending elementary school and working with my father in the crescent that we would catch rides with many men who would stop at Tommy Welch's Shell station for gas. During this period, Welch was the only service station on the island.

Steve worked at the station changing oil, pumping gas, changing spark plugs and performing other minor repairs on cars' engines. He also drove the station tow truck when needed. The Shell station once sat at old Folly Road and Maybank Highway; Steve and his family lived in one of the McLeod slave cabins throughout the 1950s.

Coleman Forest (1895) and his wife Janie (1894) had three daughters, Sarah (1923), Elizabeth (1928) and Harriet (1929); one son, Coleman Jr. (1928); and a niece, Wilimenia Grant (1916). Also living with the family were boarders Sarah Simmons (1895) and Alex Ladson (1909).

Easton Robinson (1822) and his wife Maria (1823) had two sons, Phillip (1850) and Sharper (1853); and three daughters, Rachel (1857), Rose (1860) and Celia (1866). According to Hump Urie as told to his grandson, Harry Urie, Easton Robinson was one of the slaves who was granted forty acres and a mule, only to have it taken back during the 1800s.

This picture was taken in front of Lizzie Robinson's house where she once lived. This is the very spot where the Piggly Wiggly supermarket now stands at Maybank Highway and Folly Road, across from the McLeod slaves' cabins.

Easton Robinson (1887) and his wife Elizabeth (Lizzie) Brown (1886) had four sons, Hezekiah (1919), Henry (1927), Easton (1921) and Bennie; and seven daughters, Edna (Mattie) (1915), Nellie (1912), Mary E. (1926), Ethel, Josephine, Lela and Emily.

Lizzie Robinson and Harold Richardson. *Family photograph.*

CONVERSATIONS WITH EDNA ROBINSON RICHARDSON

During interviews and conversations over the past several years with Edna Robinson Richardson, the daughter of Lizzie Robinson, she said,

> *Frazier, our family grew up on McLeod Plantation, in the house that once stood on the property where the Piggly Wiggly shopping center now stands at Maybank Highway and Folly Road. My mother worked for the McLeod family doing domestic work. When I was a young girl growing up, I recall washing and ironing clothes for Willie McLeod's family. I also worked on the farm like everyone else.*
>
> *I recall on many days, I went with my daddy on the farms. The men would dig white potatoes out of the grounds with pitchfork and would place them in baskets. I worked on several farms, Willie McLeod's, Ellis's and John Myers's, while I was a young girl. Myers's farm was located in the Riverland Terrace area next to McLeod. Cotton, green beans, butter beans and potatoes were some of the vegetables we picked. There was a time when I was expected to milk the cows my family raised. My brothers in order to get out of milking the cows would tell my parents that the cow gave more milk when I milk them. We all had a big laugh about that explanation.*
>
> *I just could not stand bending over all day picking lima beans. I told my mother I was getting a domestic job and that is what I did! Talking with my grandmother, Lea Brown, she told me they [slaves] walked to Charleston barefoot with rags wrapped around them. Most of the time, they walked blindfold. She did not know where they came from. They were auctioned off at the slave market in Charleston*

and sold to the McLeod Plantation. I really think our peoples were ashamed to talk about the way they were treated during slavery.

Frazier, my grandfather was friends of Julius and Sadie Fielding, owners of Fielding Funeral Home. During the early 1900s, Julius and his family used to visit our house regularly, especially during the Christmas holiday. My father used to go into the woods and get the bushes with the red berries during the Christmas holiday for the Fieldings.

When my father died, he was the first black buried in a vault on James Island, given to the family by Julius Fielding. He was buried in the Seabrook Cemetery on Secessionville Road, near Camp Road. My mother helped raise a lot of the young boys as boarders in our home during those years.

The 1930 census does show the following men living in the Robinson household: Joseph Delaney, Allen Brown, James Brisbane, James Fleming, Oley Brown and Jack Delaney.

Phillip Robinson (1850) and his wife Harriet (1852) had one daughter, Rinda (1887); two sons, Phillip Jr., (1894) and Hezekiah (1896); one granddaughter, Emily Brisbane (1903); six grandsons, James (1907), James Farr (1907), Jacob Farr (1890), John Farr (1903), Isaac Farr (1904) and William Monroe (1907); all were listed as mulattos.

John Richardson Sr. (1910) and his wife Edna Mattie (1915) had four sons, John Jr., Benjamin, Theodore and Samuel Richardson; and three daughters, Aletha Richardson Singelton, Harriett Richardson Bright and Mary Richardson Hawkins.

I knew the Richardson family most of my life growing up on James Island. Mrs. Richardson was affectionately called Mattie by those who were close to her. Her son John Jr. and I became close friends over the years. John Jr. is one of the past masters of Sons of Elijah Lodge, of which I am also a member. I had the privilege of talking with Mattie on numerous occasions over the years.

As I sat in her house talking with her over the years, I found her to be a pleasant and very religious person who always had something good to say about everyone. In fact, Mattie is among the last group of black women and men on the island that believes in that traditional old-time religion that many of us were raised under.

While sitting in her kitchen, she said,

Frazier, John and I got married in 1936, and he was fortunate enough to get a job at the Charleston Naval Shipyard during those hard times. John worked at the shipyard until he retired. We were fortunate enough with God's help to build this house here and raise our children. As you know, I had four sons and three daughters. Two of my sons, Theodore and Samuel, have gone home to be with the Lord. Frazier, it was one of the hardest times in my life. Both died so young and close together.

John and I believe in God, and in doing the right thing by treating people the way we wanted to be treated. I joined Payne RMUE Church and John joined First Baptist Church where he became a deacon and chairman of the board. I also did my share of work in the church and community. I really believe prayer and believing in God brought us through those hard and difficult times to the point where we are today.

John Richardson Sr. was one of the founders of the Son of Elijah Masonic Lodge #457, the fifty-six men associations, and a patron of the Daughter of Elijah Eastern Star #337, on James Island. Edna is also a member of the Daughters of the Order of Eastern Star #337. The Sons of Elijah Lodge #337 was organized and received its charter as a member of Prince Hall Grand Lodge in Columbia, South Carolina, in 1955.

Joseph Robinson (1844) and his wife Elizabeth (1847) had two daughters, Lydia (1882) and Clara (1884); and two sons, Murphy (1890) and McKever (1892).

Robert Robinson (1810) and his wife Sylvia (1820) had three sons, Cuffy (1854), Thomas (1859) and Robert (1859); and one daughter, Cinderella (1856). Thomas and Robert were twins.

Phillip Robinson (1902) and his wife Mollie (1902) had two daughters, Sarah (1916) and Harriett (1917); two sons, Phillip Jr. (1922) and Ellis (1923); and stepson Joseph Gathers (1912).

Pompey "Hardtime" Dawson (1821) and his wife Judy (1835) had two sons, William (1840) and Titus (1848); and one daughter, Mima (1851). Pompey was known by his nickname, "Hardtime," according to Hump Urie Sr., as told to his grandson, Harry Urie.

Hardtime was one of the slaves given thirty-six acres that were later taken and returned to the McLeod Plantation owners. According to other slaves, Hardtime would sing that old time Negro song "Motherless Chillins See a Hardtime" as he worked in the fields, and that is how he got his nickname, "Hardtime Dawson."

Solomon "Saul" Delaney Sr. (1843) and his wife Sallie (1845) had two daughters, Hannah (1869) and Janie; and one son, Saul (1870–1929). Also living with the family during the 1910 census were two grandsons, James (1902) and Arthur (1904); and two granddaughters, Barbara (1900) and Dollie (1906).

Mr. Saul Delaney is listed among the founding fathers of Payne Church and was a Sunday school teacher. Solomon "Saul" Delaney Sr. (1843) and his second wife Lizzie (1895) had one daughter, Anna (1914).

Solomon "Saul" Delaney Jr. (1870) and his wife Jane (1876) had one daughter, Laura (1897). Saul Delaney and his father are buried in the Dill Slave Cemetery on Riverland Drive.

Joseph Delaney Sr. (1884) and his wife Catharine R. (1892) had two sons, Christopher (Jack) (1911) and Joseph Jr. (1905); and one daughter, Sarah (1908–1976).

Christopher "Jack" Delaney (1911) and his wife Carrie Bell had two sons, Christopher and William Bennett; and three daughters, Deloris Bennett, Sarah and Betty Bennett. Jack was one of the original fifty-six men who help organized the Sons of Elijah Masonic Lodge #457 on James Island in 1955, and was a member of Payne RMUE Church.

Joe Heyward (1844) and his wife Carrie (1860) had two sons, Joseph (1882) and Josiah (1888); and four daughters, Sarah (1885), Rita (1884), Viola (1893) and Mary E. (1897). Joseph Heyward is listed as one of the founding fathers of Payne Church.

THE RIVERS
PLANTATION OWNERS

JOHN RIVERS (1783) AND HIS wife Sarah E. (1793) had one daughter, Ellenor C. Rivers Dill (1824). Also living with the family was Joseph T. Dill (1822), Ellenor's husband.

William Horace Rivers (1818) and his wife Sarah (1817) had four sons, William (1839), Charles (1844), Elias L. (1839) and Constant (1850); and three daughters, Susan (1846), Sarah (1848) and Ella (1849). Charles Rivers was a lifelong resident of James Island. Elias L. Rivers was a Confederate captain and leading authority on sea-island cotton. Constant Rivers was a Charleston County coroner.

The Rivers Plantation included that area stretching from the Ellis Plantation to Folly Road, and surrounded by Camp Road where the Payne RMUE Church and the Rivers Point subdivision apartments now stand.

The slave schedule from 1850 to 1860 shows that the Rivers family owned forty two slaves, including twelve mulattos, during these years.

SLAVES AND THEIR DESCENDANTS RESIDING ON THE RIVERS PLANTATION

Peter Brown (1840) and his wife Leia (1856) three daughters, Mariah (1870), Rebecca and Elizabeth (Lizzie) (1886).

Edna (Mattie) R. Richardson (1914), the granddaughter of Leia and Peter, said,

> *Frazier, over the years, from the time I was a little girl visiting my grandma on the Rivers Plantation, she told me and other family members that she and several other slaves walked to Charleston from a place far away. She did not know where, or the name of the place they came from. They walked through dense woods, swamps and canal; there were no roads, only trail and footpath. During their journeys, when they came to rivers that were too deep and wide to walk across, the slaves' Massa would use rowboats to ferry them across.*
>
> *While the slaves walked, the Massa rode horse and wagon. Grandma said they walked barefoot. During the journey in the daytime, the older men and women were*

Edna "Mattie" Richardson. *Family photograph.*

blindfolded to keep them from escaping. When they finally reached Charleston, most of the slaves' feet were bruised, raw and swollen; they used rags, paper and whatever they could get to put on them.

Grandma said her parents were sold to the Rivers Plantation. I think Grandma met Peter Brown, my grandpa, on the Rivers or the Lawton Plantation, and they got married. They used to live in the area behind Payne Church, next to the Smalls' creek, near Lawton Bluff; that's where I use to visit Grandma Leia. I never knew Grandpa Peter. He died when I was a little girl. Grandma Leia came to live with Mama after Grandpa died. Grandma Leia died in 1933.

March Deleston (1856) and his wife Sally (1856) had four sons, Franklin (1881), Joe (1884), William (1882) and Simon (1880); one daughter, Elizabeth (1886); a sister, Belle (1854); and a niece, Mary.

Rubin Prioleau (1896) and his wife Katie (1896) had three sons, Ben (1930), Willie (1921) and William (1923); and four daughters, Gladys (1918), Marguerite (1925), Katie (1927) and Dorothy (1930).

Jake Fergerson (1902) and his wife Viola (1906) had two daughters, Julia (1922) and Ulabelle (1923); and one son, Rubin (1925).

Abram Blake (1878) and his wife Wilhmenia Lawton (1887) had four daughters, Inez (1909), Elizabeth (1913), Anita (1919) and Martha (1920); and seven sons, Abraham (1911), Richard (1924), James (1917), Ben (1929), Elias (1922), Waring (1925) and Leroy (1927); all were listed as mulattos.

Isaac Green (1882) and his wife Eva (1890) had three daughters, Bertha (1914), Stella (1915) and Elizabeth (1922); and three sons, Isaac (1925), James and William (1930).

Isabelle Forester (1885) had two daughters, Henrietta (1915) and Katie (1918).

THE SEABROOK
PLANTATION OWNERS

WILLIAM SEABROOK (1839) WAS MARRIED to Elizabeth Seabrook (1844). The Seabrook Plantation included that area where Payne RMUE Church is located on Camp Road to the Rivers Plantation, and that section where the Old Slave Cemetery is located on Secessionville Road, and the area known as White House Plantation, between Fort Johnson Road and Camp Road, bound by Dills Bluff Road.

The slave schedule from 1850 to 1860 shows that the Seabrook family owned 195 slaves, including 22 mulattos, during these years. The slave schedule prior to the Seabrooks' ownership of this farm shows that Edward and Marion Freer owned this plantation with twenty-three slaves before selling it to the Seabrooks.

SLAVES AND THEIR DESCENDANTS RESIDING ON THE SEABROOK PLANTATION

Prince "Pappy" White (1830) and his wife Lavinia (1832) had five sons, Middleton (1854), Amos (1859), Stephen (1850), Gabriel (1864) and Prince Jr. (1867).

Middleton White (1854) was married to Phyllis Brown White (1847), who had two daughters, Martha and Anna Brown, by her first husband, Abraham Brown. After the death of Abraham Brown, Middleton married Phyllis. After the death of Phyllis, Middleton married Lizzie Brown White.

Middleton White (1854) and his second wife, Elizabeth (Lizzie) Brown White (1878), had four sons, Westmore (1900), Franklin (1912), Arthur and Eddie; and five daughters, Livinia, Jennie, Ester, Diana (1912) and Aida White Moore (1914).

Aida White Moore (1914–2005) and her husband Reverend John H. Moore (1914) had two sons, Arthur (1934) and John H. Jr. (1940); and three daughters, Rosa Lee (1932), Lois (1936, and Elizabeth (1938).

CONVERSATIONS WITH AIDA WHITE MOORE

During several interviews with Mrs. Aida White Moore, I sat at her kitchen table listening to her as she told stories about her life. I could not help being fascinated and overwhelmed by the knowledge she possessed on the history of James Island.

Aida said,

My daddy, Middleton White, and granddaddy, Pappy White, were slaves. Pappy was the overseer on the Seabrook Plantation. My daddy said that Pappy White was brought in from Wadmalaw Island to the slave market in Charleston on a boat. He was of Indian descent and looked white. He said that Mrs. Seabrook went to the slave market in Charleston to buy slaves to help with the farm after her husband was killed in the Confederate war. My grandpa, Pappy White, was bought by Mrs. Seabrook to be the overseer and run the farm. During slavery all of my daddy's brothers were sold to different plantations. Prince White Jr. was the youngest of Granddaddy's brothers. He was called "Princy." He was sold to the Grimball Plantation. My daddy stayed on the Seabrook Plantation with his daddy, Pappy White.

Grandpa and Pappy's cabin was built close to the slave master's house in case she needed him. The rest of the cabins on the plantation were lined up in a row around the plantation usually at the edge of the woods in that area between Dills Bluff Road, Fort Johnson Road and Secessionville Road.

I was born on the Seabrook Plantation. We lived on the section known as Whitehouse Plantation. I recall about twenty-four houses were there, but it could have been more. Grandpa had to make sure the slaves got up in the morning to do their work. Before going in the fields, the slave had to water and feed the mule and cows, then milk the cows before going in the field.

When I was a young girl working on the farm, they were no tractors to plow the fields. The men used mules to plow the fields and pitchforks and rakes to dig and pry under the potato plants to shake the dirt and bush loose from the potatoes and put them in crates. They also planted cotton, string beans, white potatoes, sweet potatoes, cabbages and collard greens on the plantation. I tell you, it was hard work bending over all day in the hot sun and cold.

My daddy said during slavery although they wore chains around their ankle and neck, the slaves would walk miles to get to a prayer meeting. The slaves had certain signal in songs they sing. When they sing that song, "There's a meeting tonight on the old camp ground" everyone knew there was a service that night. Pappy, his family and the other slaves on the plantation hold prayer meetings in a bush tent near the river called "Will Foot Run." The bush tent was made with small tree branches and lined with paper bags. They used crates and boxes for seats.

If there was trouble, the people would sing that song "Nobody Know the Trouble I Seen" and when time to quit work, "Swing Low Sweet Chariot," time to get paid, "When the Roll is Called Up Yonder," when time to eat, "We Will Break Bread

Aida White Moore. *Family photograph.*

Together;" when sick, "O God Our Help in Ages Past" and for service, "Praise God from Whom all Blessing Flow."

All the plantations had their share of mulatto children. We knew that the white farmers were having sex with the black women, but that was a subject you did not ask question or talk about. When a half-white child show up in a family the white farmer would pay unusual attention to that one and made sure the child was taken care of. Daddy said during slavery two black men had a baby with white women one was caught and killed.

We had several fig, pear, peach and plum trees in our yard. My sisters and I would pick the fruit of the trees and the black berries that grew wild to help my daddy with expenses. During farming season he would take the fruits and vegetables to Seabrook's Boat Landing in his wagon with his mule pulling it.

At the landing, Daddy would unhitch the mule from the wagon and load the vegetables on the ferry boat, and ride to Charleston market. He would sell his vegetables and fruit. Sometimes I would go with him to sell the vegetables; I like to ride the big ferry boat to Charleston. When we were young, all the children had to attend Sunday school every Sunday. I remember my Sunday school teacher was Ben Judge he would always let me sit at the front of the class and call on me to read the Bible to the rest of the children.

Mr. Judge would compliment me telling my daddy how smart I was in Sunday school. Before daddy died he told me one of the white men on the Seabrook's Plantation was Ben Judge's daddy. I don't want to call the name but it was one of the plantation owners. Frazier, just looking at the Judges you could tell their parents were white.

Daddy said it was rare that a slave master allowed their slaves to learn to read, but Mrs. Janie Seabrook taught Pappy and other slaves and their children on her plantation to read and write because she wanted them to get a little education even though they were slaves. Daddy said he thought she was a good person because she took interest in all of her slaves. Daddy said the Seabrooks were the only plantation that he knew of on James Islands where slaves were allowed to read and write.

Daddy said at the end of slavery, in 1868, the head of some of the slave families were given forty acres and a mule. Daddy said the slaves got a mule and land through the Freedmen Bureau by the government at Willie McLeod's Plantation. He said later the land that was given to the slaves were taken, and given back to the plantation owner. Daddy said Mrs. Seabrook and her daughter took Grandpa Pappy White to church with them on Sunday. The church stood where the St. Matthew Episcopal Church now stands on Camp Road near the Richardson property.

After the slaves were free, in 1867, Mrs. Seabrook decided to let Pappy and the other slaves on her plantation have the land where they held prayer meetings. In 1875, Pappy White and the former slaves christen the platform for the church. Because of his religious background, Grandpa organized and helped build the first African American Methodist Church and became the first minister of what is now Payne RMUE Church on Camp Road, James Island.

My daddy met my mother, Elizabeth Brown, on the Seabrook Plantation. She was working doing domestic work for the Seabrooks. They got married. After the death of

First Payne RMUE Church on Camp Road. *Family photograph.*

Pappy White, my daddy moved to Stiles Bee Plantation and became the overseer and foreman for them.

Frazier, I was an historian and researcher in Payne Church, and held many position; historical records shows that the property where our present Payne RMUE Church stands on Camp Road, by the large ditch, separated the Seabrook Plantation from the Rivers Plantation. The property was sold to my grandpappy and the rest of the free slave in 1875, by Mrs. Janie Seabrook, for one dollar a year for ninety-nine years.

Her only stipulation was that the land be used for religious purposes. I went to Three Trees Elementary School on Fort Johnson Road; the school was a three-room board building. I remember that building. It was high up off the ground. Many times I would hide under the school in fear the teacher would beat me. A girl named Lena Seabrook got beat every day by Miss Sanny Green, our teacher.

One day I hid under the school, Mrs. Green asked my sister Isadora why I was not in school. She told her and she called to me, "Come out from under there Aida, why are you hiding?" I said that I did not want to get beat. She told me, "If you just do what I tell you, you won't get beat. Your friend Lena gets beat because she failed to listen." Frazier the schoolbook that the state supplies to the school was used first by the white school and then passed down to the Negro school.

When I finished elementary school, there was no high school on James Island for Negros, that's what black people were called in those days. I went to live with my sister in the city of Charleston. I attended Burke Industrial School until I graduated. Daddy provided money for me to go to college, but due to unfortunate circumstances, I was not able to go.

I got married to John in 1934, and moved to the Honey Hill section, that where my husband and I raise our children. My husband John and I bought a half-acre of land from the Clarks for fifty dollars. I am proud of all my children and their accomplishments, but I am especially proud of Rosa Lee. She is a teacher and about to retire.

I am looking forward to spending time with her and doing some traveling together even if it is no further than around Charleston. That if the good Lord let me live to do that, otherwise, Frazier, I have enjoyed my life on this earth and God is still blessing me. Just look at what you are doing for James Island—telling the history of our trial and tribulations and how we overcome slavery to this day, Amen, thank God.

Frazier, I remember some of the men that were slaves on the plantation. William Seabrook, Scipio Singelton, Jerry Drayton, Mallard Drayton, Peter Brown, John McKelvey, Henry Fergerson, Edward Green, Demos Walton and Willington White. These men were listed as receivers of the property given to them by Mrs. Seabrook, where Payne Church sits on Camp Road today.

Aida White Moore was truly one of the matriarchs of James Island. It was a privilege for me to have met her and place her name in this book as a remembrance of her valuable contribution to the historical documentation of the life and times of the people who helped to make the wilderness of James Island into a home for both the slaves and their descendants.

Edward Green (1820) and his wife Christina (1829) had three sons, Aaron (1848), James (1857) and Frank (1859); and two daughters, Susan (1854) and Rose Ann (1861). Edward Green and his family were slaves on the Seabrook Plantation under overseer Pappy White. Following slavery, he was among the founding fathers of Payne Church.

Franklin Judge Sr. (1891) and his wife Josephine (1893) had six daughters, Verna Lee (1918), Amanda (1919–2003), Elizabeth (1921), Francena (1924), Julia M. (1928)

Francena Judge Backman. *Family photograph.*

and Joann; and three sons, Franklin Jr. (1926), Clarence and Harris (1929). Franklin Judge Sr. was listed as a mulatto.

Ben Judge (1884) and his wife Cornelia (1883) had one son, Gilbert (1904); one daughter, Anna Judge Richardson (1906); son-in-law Liger Richardson (1901); granddaughters Cornelia Richardson (1926) and Emmy Richardson (1928); and a boarder, Mary Richardson (1926). All were listed as mulattos. Ben Judge was listed as a leader and Sunday school teacher in Payne RMUE Church on Camp Road.

William Seabrook (1875) and his wife Betty (1878) had four daughters, Mertie (1898), Nenie (1908), Mary (1920) and Mattie (1924); and one son, William (1899).

William Seabrook (1879) and his wife Catherine (1885) had five daughters, Henrietta (1907), Julia (1909), Lena (1911), Nellie (1913) and Mary (1914); and two sons, George (Joshie) (1916) and Jerry (1919).

William (Melt) Seabrook (1911–1997) and his wife Mary had two sons, William Jr. and Theodore; and three daughters, Thelma, Albertha and Ruby.

George (Joshie) Seabrook (1916) and his wife Anna Smith (1913) had four sons, George, Harry, Joe and Leonard; and four daughters, Mary, Willa Mae, Katherine and Joe Ann.

W. Washington (1867) and his wife Nancy (1881) had seven sons, Isaac (1901), Jacob (1904), Jessie (1909), Ezekiel (1905), Alonzo (1906), Jesse (1908) and Rollie (1910); and four daughters, Estelle (1913), Eleanor (1915), Catherine (1917) and Evelyn (1921).

Aaron White (1894) and his wife Sarah (1895) had three daughters, Bettie (1920), Naomi (1923) and Francis (1928); Sarah White is listed among the founding mothers of Payne Church.

Alexander Mack (1000) and his wife Mary (1891) had four sons, Alexander Jr. (1918), Isaac (1919), Joseph (1920) and Kit (1926); and four daughters, Mary (1917), Lillian (1923), Esolina (1916) and Thelma (1929).

Aleck Mack (1885) and his wife Mary (1885) had four daughters, Nuda (1909), Maria (1911), Essie (1913) and Mary (1915); and two sons, Aleck (1917) and Isaiah (1919).

Phillip Guest (1855–1915) and his wife Sophia (1860) had one daughter, Ella (1892); and one son, Isaac (1881–1958). Sophie Guess was listed as one of the founding mothers of Payne Church in 1875.

Isaac Guest (1881–1958) and his wife Nancy (1881) had one daughter, Ruth (1913); sister-in-law, Daisy Attles (1914); and mother-in-law, Caroline Attles (1870).

Alfred Attles (1858) and his wife Cornelia (1860) had one son, Joseph (1882); and two daughters, Nancy (1884) and Sarah (1898).

Abram Brown (1895) and his wife Elsey (1900) had five sons, Abram, Cecil (1914), Frank (1916), Richard (1918) and Andes (1927), and one daughter, Mary (1920).

Sam Prioleau (1890) and his wife Liza (1893) had four sons, John W. (1911), Ben (1913), Joe (1915) and Woodrow (1919); and one daughter, Liza (1926).

Stephen Gibbs (1843) and his wife Kate (1840) had one daughter, Patty. Also living with the family were Patti Geddis (1850), Sybbey Geddis (1854) and Mollie Geddis (1862).

Following the end of slavery, Elizabeth Seabrook, owner of the Seabrook Plantation, gave the property to the free slaves where the church now stands on Camp Road. In 1875, Reverend Pappy White was listed as the church's first pastor. Numerous preachers have served since its existence. Some of the pastors were Reverend Richard Brown, Reverend Bernard Brown, Reverend Joseph U. Grant, Reverend James Blake, Reverend Arthur Blunt, Reverend John H. Moore, Reverend Hercules Champagne and the present pastor, Reverend Joseph Powell.

The Legare
Plantation Owners

Tʜᴇ sʟᴀᴠᴇ sᴄʜᴇᴅᴜʟᴇ ꜰʀᴏᴍ 1850 to 1860 shows the Legare family owned two hundred slaves, including thirty mulattos, during these years. According to the slaves and oral history passed down through the generations, the Legare family rented their slaves out to other plantations as hired hands.

Sʟᴀᴠᴇs ᴀɴᴅ Tʜᴇɪʀ Dᴇsᴄᴇɴᴅᴀɴᴛs Rᴇsɪᴅɪɴɢ ᴏɴ ᴛʜᴇ Lᴇɢᴀʀᴇ Pʟᴀɴᴛᴀᴛɪᴏɴ

John Richardson (1848) and his wife Emma (1841) had two sons, Jacob (1881) and James (1890), and a daughter, Blossom (1881).

James Richardson Sr. (1890) and his wife Carrie (1893) had five sons, John (1910), Harold (1919), James Jr. (1921), William (1923) and Louis; and four daughters, Marie (1915), Emma (1913), Melvena (1917) and Pearl (1927).

Like most men on James Island during this era, James supported his family by farming. Records reveal that James was drafted in the U.S. Army in 1918, and fought during World War I.

A letter and an envelope dated August 12, 1918, was mailed to his wife Carrie, in reference to his five-dollar monthly allotment check. It was written by a sergeant Harry Everett. Carrie also received a letter from President Richard Nixon honoring the memory of James Richardson for service to his country during World War I.

Joseph Richardson (1878) and his wife Heita (1876) had one son, Benjamin (1896); and two daughters, Carrie (1898) and Rebecca (1899).

Irwin Richardson (1859) and his wife Jane (1860) had four sons, Nelson (1890), Irwin Jr. (1891), Frank (1880) and Joseph (1903); and one daughter, Victoria (1894).

Baker Richardson (1889–1935) and his wife Julia (1891) had four sons, Robert (1911), Daniel (1912), Alfred (1913) and James (1917); and four daughters, Julia (1915), Bunch (1919), Rosa (1921) and Sallie. All were listed as mulattos.

James Richardson. *Family photograph.*

Toby Richardson (1882) and his wife Mary (1885) had three sons, Noble (1910), Clarence (1921) and Richard (1912); two daughters, Posey (1912) and Mattie (1917); a daughter-in-law, Irene (1913); and grandson Leon Gilliard.

Marshall Singelton (1883) and his wife Lula are buried in the slave cemetery near the intersection of Fort Lamar Road and Battalion Drive. This is near the site where the Civil War was fought at Secessionville on June 16, 1862.

Heritage Trust, a part of the S.C. Department of Natural Resources Habitat Protection Section, acquired the 13.5-acre Fort Lamar Heritage Preserve in 1996. The preserve includes ramparts from Fort Lamar, a battery that helped repel Union troops during the Battle of Secessionville on June 16, 1862.

Toby Singelton (1910) and his wife Wilhelmina Chavis (1911) had three children, Kathleen, Catherine and George R.C. Toby was one of the original fifty-six men who helped organize the Sons of Elijah Lodge on James Island, and was one of its past masters. He was a member and an elder at St. James Presbyterian Church and was considered a pillar in the community.

Abraham "Man" Singelton (1897–1965) and his wife Mary (1901) had three sons, Harold (1920), Josiah (1928) and James (1926); three daughters, Anna (1928), Bernice (1929) and Grace; and Abraham's mother, Sarah (1863), a widow who resided with them.

Abraham Singelton was known in the Sol Legare community by his nickname, "Man." Although he was married, records in the archives revealed that he killed a female on Sol Legare by stabbing her to death on Mosquito Beach. He was said to have been having an affair with the victim, Victoria Davis Wilder, according to many of the old-timers on James Island, including my father. I remember my father coming home and telling my mother and grandmother that Victoria had been killed by Man.

Several people on Sol Legare said that on the night of the killing, the victim was heard screaming and begging for help while she was being assaulted. No one would open their door or go to her aid; her body was discovered several days later in a bush on Mosquito Beach.

According to O'Neil Wilder, Sandy Brown and many others, Man had a mean streak and no one crossed or messed with him. Records show he spent several years in prison for the murder. Victoria was the sister of Fredrick Davis of the Grimball Plantation and the wife of Mosey Wilder. I was young at the time but recalled that she was a very attractive woman who many men admired.

Calvin Chavis (1918) and his wife Mamie R. had six sons, Calvin Jr., George R., Gene, Joseph Remus, Thomas and Malcolm Chavis; and four daughters, Emma L., Hermenia, Deloris and Geraldine.

CONVERSATIONS WITH MAMIE R. CHAVIS

I sat in the front room of Mamie Chavis's house with her and listened as she talked about her life growing up. It immediately became apparent that she was a religious

Mamie Chavis. *Family photograph.*

and proud black woman. Mamie is among the last blacks on the island who deeply believed in a tradition known as that "old-time religion." This meant before you could become a member of one of the churches on the island, you would have to go out into the wilderness and pray and be led by the spirit into the church.

She said,

Frazier, let me tell you about me. When I was a little girl growing up, every morning between four and five o'clock, our parents would make sure my sisters, brothers and I got up. Before going to school every morning, we walked through woods and the footpath on the edge of marshes all the way to get to Peas Island and later to Folly Beach to Massenburg Shrimp Dock. Junius Richardson was captain of one boat; he was the headman for Massenburg Shrimp Company.

As the shrimp boats came into the dock, the men would empty the net. We would head shrimp for about two hours. If you know anything about heading shrimp that meant you hold a handful of shrimp in each hand. Then you would use the thumb and fourth finger to pluck the head of the shrimp. When it was time, we walked back through the woods, marshes, bushes and the footpath the men from Sol Legare made. At home, we would bathe in a three-foot tin tub our mother used to wash our clothes in. During the winter months, we would heat the water in the chimney fireplace then we would go to the three-room school here on Sol Legare. At the end of the school day, and on Saturday, each of us would take a basket of vegetables like string beans, corns, potatoes, collard green, okra and many others to sell on Folly Beach. Sometimes when we were tired and hungry and didn't sell any vegetables, we would go to Sprawley's Restaurant on Folly Beach. He had these stale bread and cake that was ready to go back to the bakery in Charleston. We would trade some of the vegetables for the bread and cake to eat.

You know after the bridge was built between Folly Beach and James Island, we still had to pay a ten-cent toll to cross the bridge even if you walked across. Many times I went in the creek with my daddy to fish, crab and pick oysters to sell to help pay the bills. My daddy was a farmer and among the vegetables he planted was cotton.

Frazier, I tell you I hated looking down them long rows of cotton bending my back over all day. My daddy planted cotton for many years until the price fell and was no longer able to make a profit so he quit. After I was old enough, I started doing domestic work. I worked for several people over the years on Folly Beach, Secessionville Road, Riverland Drive and in the city of Charleston.

I got married in 1942, boy was I glad. I thought I finally got away from farming that's what I thought. Calvin's family was also doing farming work, I found myself right back doing the same thing. Nine days after Calvin and I got married, he was drafted in the army. Frazier, during those hard and trying times we survived because we believed in God and treated everyone the way we wanted to be treated.

Mamie is a member and a deacon in the St. James Presbyterian Church.

As I reflected on my conversations with Mamie and the other women, I could not help but feel that I was being taken back in time. It was a time when the majority of blacks on James Island was poor and appreciated simple things such as the ability to eat two meals a day. It was a time when we clung to our religious belief in God in order to survive during those turbulent years of manual labor working in the cold, rain and hot sun to earn enough money for the bare necessities of life.

William M. Wilder (1865) and his wife Sally (1885) had four daughters, Rosa (1892), Sarah (1910), Mary (1912) and Martha (1916); two granddaughters, Elizabeth Murray (1918) and Ernestine Murray (1922); and two grandsons, William M. Murray (1920) and James Murray (1924).

Theodore Wilder (1860) and his wife Elizabeth (1860) had two sons, Elijah (1880) and Peter (1882); and five daughters, Sarah (1884), Maggie (1886), Susan (1887), Nellie (1892) and Oral Belle (1897).

Andrew Wilder (1876) and his wife Mary (1881) had five sons, Harrison (1907), Josiah (1912), Thomas (1915), Andrew (1915) and Samuel (1921).

From the 1920s to the 1950s, African Americans had no public places on James Island to socialize or gather for any type of recreation. Several black men on Sol Legare decided to start a business on property their ancestors owned. These businesses were called "juke joints" and "piccolo joints." Some of the men operating these businesses were Jack Walker, Erwin Singelton, James Lafayette, William (Bubba) Chavis, Sandy Brown and Apple Wilder, among others.

Andrew (Apple) Wilder (1915) and his wife Laura Singelton Todd (1922) had two daughters, Linda Todd and Cassandra Singelton Roper; and three sons, Richard Singelton, Woodrow Singelton and Robert Wilder.

Apple and his wife, Laura, operated the Board Walk Club. They built it over the water and marsh. The second building was closed in but both buildings had space for dancing. I remember the men and women dancing on Mosquito Beach during the 1940s. They called the dance "the Charleston" and "shagging." Ironically, it is the same dance that white people in Charleston now call beach music and the shag.

Harold Singelton (1920) and his wife Ethelyn Grant had four sons, Harold Jr., Marcus, Eddie and Augustus; and four daughters, Carolyn, Marilyn, Elvira and Jacqueline. Harold was known in the community by his nickname, "Yankee."

Harold served in the U.S. Army during World War II and was honorably discharged in 1942. Like many men from Sol Legare, he once owned an oyster house business. He was later employed by the Charleston Naval Shipyard for twenty-eight years before he retired. Harold was a member of St. James Presbyterian Church and one of the original fifty-six founders of the Sons of Elijah Masonic Lodge on James Island.

Edward Singelton (1882) and his wife Catharine (1887) had six sons, Toby (1910), Dan (1915), Henry (1915), Irvin (1917), James (1925) and Isaac (1919); four daughters, Ida (1909), Elizabeth (1912), Laura (1922) and Joeflan; a grandson, Lucian (1927); and two, granddaughters, Vernleen (1928) and Johanna (1929). Catherine was listed as a mulatto.

Jerry Lefft (1880) and his wife Rosa (1888) had three sons, Hezekiah (1909), Lawrence (1908) and Nelson (1913); and three daughters, Florence (1907), Lottie (1914) and Elouise (1920).

Andrew "Apple" Wilder. *Family photograph.*

Florence Lefft Walker (1907) and her husband Joe Walker had three daughters, Gloria, Josephine and Louise; and two sons, Toby and Nelson. Mrs. Florence said,

Frazier, I remember when every road on this island was dirt. When I was a little girl, my sisters Elouise, Lottie and me would go crabbing, pick oyster and fishing with my grandpa. We also had to go on the farms, pick cotton, beans, potatoes, corn, cabbages, peas and collard greens, like all the other girls and boys.

Those were hard times. The plantation owners paid us one cent a pound to pick cotton. In those days, I was known as a tomboy. Grandpa had a mule and wagon that he hauled his vegetables in. When I was a young girl, I used to ride in the wagon with him to the end of Secessionville Road at Seabrooks boat landing at the Wappoo River. Grandpa would unhitch the mule, tie him up and load his vegetable in the big ferry boat and ride the boat to Charleston. There he would sell his vegetables in the market place.

My daddy also had a farm. All he ever did was farming, fishing, crabbing, picking oyster and shrimping. I left Charleston when I was a young girl for New York to have a better life. I lived with my uncle for a while. Then I enlisted in the army. I met my husband Joe Walker in New York; Joe was from Walterboro, South Carolina. We had five children, three girls and two boys, in New York before I came back home to stay.

Ben Richardson (1898) and his wife Emma Matthew (1903) had seven sons, Ben Jr. (1924), Amos (1925), Thomas, Arthur, Fredrick, Buster (1926) and Remus (1929); and five daughters, Susie, Louise, Gracie, Lorenzo and Mamie.

Ben was best known by his nickname, "Dimmy." He was one of the men who beat the drum for Sol Legare Lodge and is shown in the photo marching in the May Day parade in 1938.

Thomas Chavis (1890) and his wife Sarah (1892) had four sons, Henry (1913), John (1915), Thomas (1921) and William (1924); and three daughters, Sarah (1917), Alice (1919) and Wilhelmina (1926).

Thomas was born and raised on the Grimball Plantation, the son of Paul Chavis. Thomas would marry Sarah and move to Sol Legare. He was a farmer and was listed as one of the founding fathers of Payne RMUE Church under the leadership of Reverend Pappy White.

Joseph Chavis (1888) and his wife Maryann (1889) had four sons, Joseph Jr. (1916), Calvin (1918), Alphonso (1926) and Raymond (1911); and three daughters, Mary (1913), Liza (1915) and Wilhelmina (1911). Joseph, the son of Paul and Betsy Chavis, was also born and raised on the Grimball Plantation. After his marriage to Maryann, he moved to Sol Legare, where he continued his farming.

Benjamin Wallace (1875) and his wife Hattie (1879) had four sons, Benjamin (1898), Henry (1896), Ernest (1906) and Eugene (1907); and one daughter, Louise (1908). Also living in the household were Lou Fordham (1884), Ella Brown (1882) and Sophia Brown (1885), all listed as mulattos.

Joseph Chavis leading his horse in front of his house.
Family photograph.

Henry Wallace (1896) and his wife Rebecca (1893) had two sons, James and Franklin Wallace (1921); and six daughters, Henrietta (1913), Mary (1918), Bernice (1923), Louise (1925), Levola (1927) and Isabelle (1929).

Ezekiel Lafayette (1865) and his wife Maggie (1885) had five daughters, Eva (1915), Tamer (1920), Dozalee, Mary and Luelyn (1928); and three sons, Oscar (1916), Edward (1921) and David (1929).

James Lafayette (1899) and his wife Sarah (1900) had five daughters, Bertha (1915), Naomi (1917), Rosa Lee (1918), Ruth (1919) and Thelma (1928); and three sons, Leon (1923), James Jr. (1925) and Rufus (1927).

George Lafayette (1919–2003) and his wife Genevieve Cromwell had four children, George Jr., Herbert, Peggy Lafayette Frazier and Georgette Lafayette Smith. George was one of the original fifty-six men who helped organize the Sons of Elijah Lodge on James Island. He was a member of St. James Presbyterian Church and served on the trustee board for several years. He was a World War II veteran. After being discharged from the army, he worked at the Charleston Naval Shipyard until he retired.

Scippio Wigfall (1867) and his wife Rebecca (1872) had two sons, Abram (1899) and Julius (1910); and two daughters, Maggie (1904) and Julie (1918).

Henry Wigfall (1906) and his wife Becky (1909) had one daughter, Loretta (1927), and one son, Henry Jr. (1925).

Ernest Wilder (1921–2004), and his wife Catharine Matthew had one daughter, Cathy. Everyone in the community affectionately called Ernest by his nickname, "Yick." I knew Yick growing up before he left for the army during World War II.

Laura Gilliard Jackson in front of her house in what is now known as Secessionville Acres. *Family photograph.*

After he returned home, he was employed by the Charleston Naval Shipyard for close to thirty years before retiring. Ernest was a member of St. James Presbyterian Church, and served on the trustee board for several years. He was a mason and an associate of the former James Hotel in Charleston, South Carolina.

Mosey Wilder was married to Victoria Davis (1893). Victoria was murdered on Sol Legare by Abraham (Man) Singelton during the 1940s.

Plenty Jackson (1860) and his wife Rina (1865) had a son, Samuel (1888). After the death of Rhina, his first wife, Plenty Jackson married Laura Gilliard.

Plenty Jackson (1860) and his second wife Laura Gilliard (1873–1947) had two daughters, Lula (1912) and Georgiana Jackson Webb (1907); son-in-law James Webb Sr. (1903); and three grandsons, James Webb Jr., (1928), Jessie F. Webb (1929) and John Wilson Jackson (1920).

Thomas Backman (1919–1964) and his wife Susie Brown (1922–1990) had six sons, Thomas Jr., Robert, Reginald, Freddie, Sammy and Richard Singelton; and one daughter, Elizabeth Backman Richardson. As a teenager, Thomas grew up on the Bees Fields section of James Island while his wife Susie grew up in the Sol Legare area of the island.

Thomas started his career fishing for a living. In 1940, he married Susie Backman and she also fished with him. At the beginning, in 1944, they fished in the local rivers of Sol Legare and the Stono River with a small boat. Then in 1952, with the purchase of a small shrimp trawler, the *Porkey*, Thomas and Susie went into business for themselves.

The business began to prosper and they opened Backman Seafood adjacent to the Sol Legare Creek. Thomas died in 1964, leaving Susie in charge. Her knowledge of the river coupled with her business savvy acquired from her husband and along with the support of her sons and daughter, Liz, Susie, in 1973, christened the business's second shrimp trawler the *Backman Elizabeth*. Her sons fished in rivers and in the ocean from Charleston to Key West, Florida, harvesting fish and crabs. The business also included oysters and clams.

The Backman Seafood business continued to prosper under the leadership of Susie. By the mid-1980s, she had a fleet of six shrimp trawlers: the *Admiral Backman*, *Backman Enterprise, Sue Backman, Elizabeth, Porkey* and the *Backman Brothers*. Over twenty employees worked for the business at any given time. Susie died in 1990, leaving the business to her sons and daughter Elizabeth, with her oldest son, Thomas Jr., as manager. The business is still operated by her son, Thomas Jr.

Joe Walker (1905) and his wife Mattie Wilder (1908) had seven sons, Walter, Josiah, Johnry, Phillip, Archie, Nathan and Hezekiah; and five daughters, Dorothy, Beulah, Shirley, Marie and Hilda.

Alonzo Gilliard (1921) is married to Suzan Gilliard. Talking with Alonzo on a number of occasions, he said to me,

> *Frazier, when I was a young boy just about everybody on Sol Legare had small farms. When the men were not working on their farms, they were fishing, picking oysters, casting for shrimps and crabbing. We lived off the land and the river in those days.*
>
> *I worked on the farms and in the creek with my family until around 1940. Then as a teenager I moved to the city of Charleston, and worked on a couple of jobs until I was hired by the cigar factory* [American Tobacco Company] *and worked there until I retired.*
>
> *A group of us, fifty-six black men from James Island to be exact, decided to organize a masonic lodge. Following an investigation into each man's background, we went through the entire masonic ritual in Charleston and were raised to the third degree of master mason. The group selected the name "Sons of Elijah Lodge." James Brook Williams was appointed the first worshipful master of the lodge, the same lodge you now belong to.*

Henry "Bim" Gilliard (1900) and his wife Nellie (1902) had two sons, Ossie (1921) and Ernest (1923); and two daughters, Mildred (1925) and Delia. I remember Henry Gilliard; he was affectionately called "Bim." He and my father were friends and worked together on George Nungezer's farm. Bim was a truck driver and every morning during the week he would come by our house to pick up my father for work.

Lawrence Gilliard (1887) and his wife Pricilla (1895) had five sons, Frank (Franklin) (1911), Isaac (1913), Jefferson (1918), Alonzo (1921) and Prince; and four daughters, Rebecca (1913), Lovey A. (1927), Marie (1929) and Pricilla (1933).

Luscious McKelvey (1909) was married to Lila McKelvey (1911). During a conversation, Lila said,

> *Frazier when I was a young girl, I worked on all the farms like the rest of the young people. I used to work at the oyster factory opening oysters. The factory*

was down there at Mosquito Beach. Things were not good for black people here in Charleston when I was young.

When I was old enough I got involved with Luscious. He used to live in the Fort Johnson area. People called that place "Down the Island." You know that's where all the McKelveys lives off Fort Johnson Road. We decided to pack up and go to New York. We lived in New York for several years before coming back home to Charleston.

Anna Walker (1898) was a widow. She had two sons, Joe and Thomas (1925); and six daughters, Isadore (1913), Martha (1912), Janie (1916), Susie (1915), Alice (1916) and Loretta (1922); granddaughters Janie Brown (1925) and Letha Brown (1927); and grandsons Walter Walker (1927), Hezekiah Walker (1928), and Willie Walker (1929).

Betty Walker (1864) was a widow. She had three daughters, Elouise (1885), Mary (1897) and Susan (1898); and six sons, Eddie (1887), Perry (1887), Allen (1891), Oscar (1897), Joseph (1895) and James (1899).

Bessie Walker (1874) was a widow. She had one son, Allan (1890); two grandsons, Jessie Walker (1920) and Joseph Singelton (1924); granddaughter Rosa Lee Singelton; and adopted son Elijah Walker.

Sylvia Walker was a widow. She had three sons, Wallace (1875), Isaac (1899) and Dandy (1899); one daughter, Rachel (1879); and three grandsons, Isaac (1878), James (1890) and William Lafayette (1897).

Oscar Walker (1897) and his wife Carrie (1902) had three sons, Cedrith (1918), Guy (1925) and Hezekiah (1927); and three daughters, Susie (1921), Maggie (1923) and Gladys (1929).

Jack Walker and his wife Diana had three sons, Jack Jr., Perry and Harold Walker; and three daughters, Hallie Walker Wright, Bertie Walker and Anna Mae Walker Rivers.

Wallie Walker (1880) and his wife Anna (1880) had six daughters, Linda (1908), Julia (1910), Isadora (1913), Susan (1914), Alice (1916) and Wilhelmina (1919); and one son, Josiah (1904).

Gabriel Wilder (1877) and his wife Carrie (1890) had two daughters, Amelia (1912) and Emma (1914); and three sons, Gabriel (1916), Nathaniel (1918) and Tom (1920).

John Wilder (1886) and his wife Christina (1888) had four sons, William (1912), Henry (1915), John (1917) and Christopher (1920); and four daughters, Hannah (1910), Martha (1909), Susie (1914) and Mary (1918).

John Wilder (1898) and his wife Lela (1900) had two sons, Ernest (1916) and Alonzo (1928); and five daughters, Bernice (1918), Ethel (1920), Marguerite (1922), Virginia (1924) and Mamie (1929).

Albert Fell (1838) and his wife Hannah had two sons, George (1868) and Robert (1869). Also living with the family were Rhino White (1854), Samuel Watson (1863) and Armetta Dennis (1839).

Leggie Fell (1835) and his wife Elizabeth (1842) had one daughter, Hester (1876); and a grandson, Julius Walker (1892).

Royal Palmer (1860–1935) and his wife Hester Fell (1876) had two sons, Edward (1919) and Julius (1924); and two daughters, Elizabeth (1916) and Mattie (1917). Mattie eventually married Lorenzo Whaley and moved to the Grimball Plantation.

Harriet Davis (1840) was a widow. She had one daughter, Betty (1878). Living with her were Cynder Lafayette (1850); a brother, Frances Moore (1840); and nieces Etta Lafayette (1890), Martha Moore (1891), Estel Ladson (1886) and Josephine Ladson (1888).

George Brown (1885) and his wife Lula (1890) had two sons, George (1915) and Boise (1923); and three daughters, Sally (1912), Franklea and Earthlee (1925).

Sam Brown (1884) and his wife Florence (1890) had four daughters, Nell (1906), Minerva (1908), Bell (1910) and Ida (1918); and two sons, Sam (1912) and Henry (1914).

William Howard (1860) and his wife Lizzie Scott (1865) had two daughters, Anna (1885) and Eliza (1888); and six sons, George (1881), Julius (1892), William (1894), Arthur (1896–1972), Amos (1898) and James (1900).

Scott Howard (1862) and his wife Lizzie had four sons, Rubin (1897), Edgar (1906), Edward (1915) and Charles (1916); and four daughters, Mabel (1919), Emma (1908), Catherine (1910) and Maggie (1912).

Wilson Jackson (1900) and his wife Susan (1904) had four daughters, Wilhelmina (1921), Beatrice (1923), Earlene (1925) and Edith (1928); and one son, John L. (1929).

A house owned by the Fergerson family at the corner of Camp and Dill Bluff Road was used as a church for worship services during the early years. The first wooden structure was built in 1869. The Reverend Green was the church's first pastor, followed by Reverend Frayer, Reverend Briton, Reverend Weston and Reverend Cooper Whaley, between the years 1869 and 1959.

In 1959, Reverend William Grant was called to be the church's pastor. Under his leadership, a new church was built and dedicated. Reverend Grant served eight years as pastor of the church. In 1971, Reverend Alex White was called to serve as pastor. He also served eight years. In July 1978, Reverend J.D. Dash was called to serve as pastor; he served for five years. In February 1985, Reverend Bernard J. Gadsden Sr., was installed as pastor. As of this writing, he is still the pastor.

THE CLARK PLANTATION OWNERS

E PHRAIM CLARK (1812) AND HIS wife Susan Clark (1815) had one daughter, Susan Jane (1837); and three sons, Archibald (1836), John L. (1849) and Edward B. (1853). Julian H. Clark (1882) and his wife Mary (1884) had three sons, William (1909), John (1911) and Julian H. (1924); and four daughters, Julia (1914), Monaca (1916), Margaret (1918) and Lavinia (1920).

The Clark Plantation starts by the Rivers Plantation and is surrounded by Camp Road, across Dill's Bluff Road, to the marsh at Wappoo Creek, including those areas known as Green Hill, Honey Hill and Dills Bluff. Most of this property was once owned by, and purchased from, Joseph Dill of the Dill Plantation.

The slave schedule from 1850 to 1860 shows the Clark family owned seventy-two slaves, including thirteen mulattos, during these years.

SLAVES AND THEIR DESCENDANTS RESIDING ON THE CLARK PLANTATION

James (Brooks) Williams (1896) and his wife Lydia F. (1898–1981) had two daughters, Lucinda (1919) and Henrietta (1921); and three sons, James Jr. (1923), Josiah (1925) and Sypio (1927). Brooks served in the United States Army during World War I and was a farmer.

During the farming and sharecropping era, Brooks was at one time the overseer on the Clark Plantation. Many of the older people working on the plantation, including Aida Moore, Cecelia Green and Eva F. McKelvey, said that Brooks did not treat the workers with compassion during those hard times.

He was known during his young age as a Casanova. Brooks Williams was one of the fifty-six men who helped organize the Sons of Elijah Masonic Lodge #457 and was appointed its first worshipful master on James Island. He was a member and an elder of St. James Presbyterian Church until his death.

Stephen White (1890) and his wife Betsy (1891) had two daughters, Evelyn (1911) and Mamie (1917); three sons, Aaron (1918), Primus (1924) and John (1927); and adopted son Stephen Jr. (1927).

Jeff Washington (1833) and his wife Lena (1840) had one son, Peter (1866); and one daughter, Lucy (1869). Also living with them was Barry Lawrence (1847).

Geoffrey Washington (1845) and his wife Lena had one daughter, Lena (1882); and one son, William (1885).

George Lemon (1878) and his wife Lena Washington (1882) had three sons, Jeffery (1910), Ephraim (1919) and Joseph (1922); three daughters, Rebecca (1913), Julia (1916) and Susan (1920); and a grandson, Peter (1921).

CONVERSATIONS WITH MY UNCLE, JAMES SMALLS, AND HIS WIFE, SUSIE LEMON SMALLS

James Smalls (1916–1999) and his wife Susie Lemon (1920–2004) had two sons, Nathaniel and Samuel; and four daughters, Lucile Smalls Hudson, Loretta Smalls Chisolm, Janie Smalls Roper and Essie Rena Smalls.

I called Uncle James by his nickname, "Scoot." As I talked with him over the years, he said,

> *Son, I was born and raised on the Dill Plantation in Turkey Pen with my two sisters, Sis and Child. When I was a boy things were pretty rough for the family. We had no stove to heat the house and cook the food in those old days. Pa and Ma used the fireplace in the chimney to cook the food and heat the house.*
>
> *When I was six years old, I started going to Cut Bridge School. You know where that is. Sis would walk my cousin, Harry Urie, and me to school. At the end of the school day, Sis would come back and walk Harry and me to the cotton field to Ma. Ma would tie croker sacks around our waist as we picked the cotton. Man, I hated bending my back all day picking cotton. Old Man King paid one cent a pound for the cotton.*
>
> *Son, we had some very hard times growing up on the Dill Plantation. Pa was the chauffeur for the Dills and the Kings. Pa use to drive the Dills and Old Man King around the plantation in a horse and buggy to check on the people working in the field. He used to clean the Dill house and yard and keep the family's graves clean. We picked cotton, beans, potatoes and tomatoes.*
>
> *When I was old enough, I cut wood for the chimney and plowed the field while Ma, Child and Sis planted the seed to grow the vegetables. They would clean around the plants with hoes and rakes. We all worked in the fields that Pa farmed when we were not busy working on the Dills' farms. When I turned twenty-one, I got married to Sue and moved into one of the slave cabin by the canal.*
>
> *Harry Urie, my cousin, lived next door with his mother, Julia Gadsden, and stepfather, Joseph Gadsden, and his grandpa, Hump Urie. I spent many evenings after*

Sue Lemon Smalls. *Family photograph.*

work watching your daddy knit cast nets for fishing. That is how I learned to make nets myself. A few years after I got married, I got a job working for Rhodes Lumber Company. I worked there until I retired.

In my conversation with Aunt Sue over the years, she said,

Son your Uncle James and I got married in July of 1940. We had some hard days on Turkey Pen on the Dill Plantation. When we moved out of the slave cabin we had very little besides the clothes on our back. You know about that because you slept with my sons, Nathan and Sam, in that old brokedown shack a few times over the years.

We moved here on this property that my parents gave to me and your uncle "Scoot." He got a job with Rhodes Lumber Company on Maybank Highway, on James Island. I got a job at the cigar factory in Charleston [American Tobacco Company].

Before Mama Lucy died she told your mother, Sis, and your Aunt Child, to make sure your Uncle Scoot married me. We had our ups and downs like many husbands and wives, but we had a wonderful life together. Son, don't let anyone fool you. The black people on James Island believe in God, prayer, have faith and worked hard during their lives. It helped us survive and prosper throughout the years. Son, I really missed Scoot since he gone home to God. The only thing for me to do is wait till my time comes and I know I will see him again.

Aunt Sue was a wonderful woman. She was easy to talk with; no matter what was on your mind she would listen and then give you sound advice that you were able to live with while at the same time making you laugh. She died in April 2004. I was saddened by her death. She was one of the few women that I could discuss problems of a confidential nature and remain at ease with. She was an aunt and a friend.

Priestly Washington (1914) and his wife Essileen had seven sons, George, Priestly, Paul, Charles, Bernard, Joseph and Robert Washington; and four daughters, Ruth, Essie, Pearl and Edna.

Pearl Washington McKelvey said,

Son my daddy Priestly was a jack of all trades. He had his own farm and at one time he worked for Charleston County government, Charleston Naval Shipyard, the Lawton and Hinson Plantations and he also worked on the Nungezer farm.

Ben Washington (1873) and his wife Emma G. (1875) had two sons, Isaac (1908) and William (1910); and three daughters, Emily (1915), Evelyn (1917) and Rosa Lee (1918).

William Washington (1885) and his wife Eliza (1890) had an adopted daughter, Louise (1914). I remember Ms. Louise Williams. During my tenure at St. James Parochial School between 1941 and 1948, she was one of our dietitians at the school. I recall she was a very beautiful and caring person.

Frank Lafayette (1890) and his wife Georgiana (1893) had five sons, Isaac (1919), John R. (1922), Jeff (1926), David (1928) and Frank Jr. (1929); and two daughters, May and Sallie.

Frank and my father worked together for several years on the Nungezer farm. From the 1920s through the 1940s, my father and Frank evidently had a close, cordial, friendly relationship. Many times when he came home from work in the evening, my father would talk about how he and Frank survived that particular day.

He talked about plowing mules, planting seeds and digging irrigation ditches in the cold and rain to water the vegetables. During the harvest season they boxed tomatoes, corns, beans, squash, collard greens, cabbages and cucumbers to be shipped by railroad to other states. I remember Frank's wife, Mrs. Georgiana. She was a short lady. I recall many times when I visited my aunt and uncle, she would be smoking her pipe. She lived in the same community as my Uncle James and Aunt Sue.

Rachel Lafayette (1941) was the granddaughter of Frank and Georgiana Lafayette. Rachel attended the St. James Parochial School with several of my sisters. During my conversations with Rachel, she said,

> Son, my grandmother did domestic work to help the family earn enough money to pay expenses while my grandfather worked on the Nungezer farm.
>
> My aunt, Louise Williams, was married to Robert Williams. They had a child that died shortly after birth. Her husband Robert died at an early age. She did domestic work for the Welch family on Stone Post Road during the 1940s. She attended beautician school in Charleston and used her home as a beauty shop.
>
> I was a young girl at the time and helped her by washing then straighten the hairs of the women with a straighten comb. Shortly afterwards, she had a beauty shop built next door to her house and ran the business from there. Her house and the beauty shop were located at the corner of Fort Johnson and Camp Road.
>
> Her house is still there across from the fire station. I left home in 1959. I first went to New York and then to Maryland. You know during those days they were very few opportunities for black people in the South. That was one of the reasons I left, to make a better life for myself, which I did. I bought a home in Maryland and worked until I retired and now I have returned home.

Jack Ladson (1817) and his wife Belle (1822) had two sons, James (1853) and Fortune (1845); and one daughter, Venus (1855). Also living with the family were Harris Ford (1857) and Margaret Ford (1862).

Fortune Ladson (1845) and his wife Polly (1850) had four sons, Henry (1883), Arthur (1884), Ephraim (1887) and Julius (1888); and three daughters, Elvira (1878), Florence (1894) and Claudia (1897).

Ephraim Ladson (1887) and his wife Alice (1889) had six daughters, Wilhmenia (1920), Elemetha (1922), Naomi (1923), Lydia (1924), Irene (1927) and Alice; and six sons, William (1925), James, Ephraim, John, Henry and Paul.

Amos Watson (1848) was married to Susan (1850). According to records from the archive and oral history, Amos Watson is listed as one of the first African American registered Democratic voters on James Island. He was also one of the militiamen on James Island known as the Hunters.

Amos Watson (1869) and his wife Dinah (1885) had seven daughters, Marguerite (1910), Rosa (1911), Evelyn (1913), Ella (1917), Nora (1922), Eartha (1923) and Florence (1925); three sons, Clinton (1922), Perry (1924) and William (1927); and two granddaughters, Louise (1929) and Bettie (1930).

Amos Watson (1903–1961) and his wife Rosa Chisolm (1906–1982) had four sons, John Amos (1930), Benjamin Bennie, Elijah Herbert and James Seabrook; and nine daughters, Viola Retta Watson Campbell (1923), Julia Mae Watson Mikell, Wilhelmena Watson Boyce (1929), Helen V. Watson Campbell, Percile L. Watson Richardson, Margaret A. Watson Grippon, Dorothy L. Watson Backman, Carolyn Watson Clark and Kathleen P. Watson Brown.

Jerry Watson (1871) and his wife Gallie (1895) had four sons, Jerry W. (1912), Henry (1919), Joseph (1923) and James (1925); four daughters, Elsey (1916), Rebecca (1922), Julia (1926) and Viola (1929); granddaughter Edith (1929); and grandson Egger (1929).

Thomas Rambert (1850) and his wife Hester (1860) had four sons, Henry (1876), Sharper (1880), Atone (1882) and Isaac (1890); and three daughters, Lila (1884), Jane (1892) and Julia (1899).

William Gardner (1827) and his wife Eva (1844) had two sons, James (1869) and William (1876); and one daughter, Catherine (1870). They are listed as mulattos.

Benny Matthews (1887) and his wife Comestine Matthews (1891) had one son, Fred (1914); and two daughters, Mary (1916) and Laura (1918). Also living with the family was Benny's grandfather, Jake "Jacob" Aiken (1850).

Buster Aiken (1860) and his wife Maria (1859) had one son, Ben (1882); and four daughters, Mary (1883), Josephine (1884), Nellie (1885) and Carrie (1887).

Joseph Scott (1854) and his wife Lena (1857) had three daughters, Lena (1877), Mary (1888) and Martha (1888); and three sons, Edward (1883), Charles (1892) and Lawrence (1896). Mary and Martha were twins.

Gillie Scott (1903) and his wife Mary Elizabeth (Hattie) (1904) had four sons, Eddie (1921), John (1926), William (1927) and James (1929); and two daughters, Harriett (1923) and Mable (1925). Also living with them was Gillie's mother, Flora Thompson (1863).

Ben Scott (1880) and his wife Fannie (1881) had four daughters, Martha (1903), Pearl (1905), Sarah and Nancy (1908); and four sons, Henry (1910), Ben (1912), Richard (1914) and Fred (1919).

William Davis (1888) and his wife Hattie (1899) had six daughters, Azalea (1914), Evelina (1916), Eleanor (1917), Mary (1925), Anna (1926) and Martha (1928); and three sons, John Wilson (1929) John Henry and Joseph (1938).

Fred Scott (1875) was married to Hettie (1878). Living with them were a niece, Hettie Whaley (1916), and nephew, Willie Simmons (1923).

THE ELLIS
PLANTATION OWNERS

D.W.D. ELLIS (1855) AND HIS wife Mary R. (1870) had a son, Dan W. Jr. (1909). Thomas B. Ellis (1884) and his wife Pearl N. (1888) had one daughter, Elizabeth N. (1920); and two sons, Thomas B. Jr. (1922) and Napier (1921).

The Ellis Plantation once stretched from the Ellis Creek Bridge on the east side of Folly Road, where Lowes Lumber Company is located, to the McLeod Plantation at Harborview Road, and then stretched from the Ellis Bridge on the south side of Folly Road to Central Park Road and south to the Dill Plantation.

SLAVES AND THEIR DESCENDANTS RESIDING ON THE ELLIS PLANTATION

Frank Green (1852) and his wife Celia (1875) had one son, Franklin (1909); one daughter, Susan (1906); three grandsons, Edward (1925), Willis (1927) and Thomas Smalls (1912); and three granddaughters, Carry Smith (1921), Celia Smith (1925) and Marguerite Smith (1926).

Charles Green (1892) and his wife Mabelle (1895) had three sons, John (1917), Willie (1920) and Elijah (1926); three daughters, Eleanor (1922), Marcella (1924) and Ethel (1929); two nieces, Jennie Heyward (1910) and Hazel Heyward (1912); and two nephews, Samuel Walker (1912) and Edward Walker (1917).

William Green (1890) and his wife Maggie (1893) had five sons, Woodie (1919), Menke (1920), Hickman (1921), Boyd (1923) and Lingo (1923); and three daughters, Charity (1925), Lucile (1928) and Alameda (1929).

Esow McKelvey (1890) and his wife Elizabeth (1890) had five sons, Andes (1912), Easton (1914), Willis (1920), Joseph (1925) and Teddy (1928); three daughters, Diana (1915), Lizzie (1916) and Tena (1924); and a niece, Anna Brown (1913).

THE LAWTON PLANTATION OWNERS

WILBORN LAWTON (1782) AND HIS wife Martha (1810) had several children: Wallace (1836), M. Juliet (1838), Paul (1845), James M., Wilborn, Allison and Robert Lawton Oswald (1850). Records and deed show that Wilborn Lawton (1782) bought "Dill Bluff" from Joseph and Sarah Dill on September 30, 1819.

According to many slaves, including Hump Urie, Stephen Forest, Daniel Smalls and Eddie Gibbs, as told to Cyrus Frazier and Harry Urie, Wallace Lawton showed no compassion to slaves and had been known to spit in their faces, slap them and call them animals.

The slave schedule from 1850 to 1860 shows the Lawton family owned 110 slaves, including 25 that were listed as mulattos, during these years.

SLAVES AND THEIR DESCENDANTS RESIDING ON THE LAWTON PLANTATION

George Brown (1810) and his wife Margaret (1820) had one son, Robert (1852); and one daughter, Betsy (1853). All were mulattos.

Rebecca Matthew Lawton Chavis (1863) was a widow. She had two daughters, Emily (1882) and Lena (1884); and three sons, Rhett (1886), Cromwell (1893) and William (1895). Following the death of her sister Betsy, Rebecca married her sister's husband, Paul Chavis, my great-grandfather.

Rhett Lawton (1886–1939) and his wife Martha (1895) had two daughters, Ellen (1910) and Sarah (1912). Records revealed that Rhett Lawton served in the U.S. Army during World War I. Upon his return from the war, people in the community called him by his nickname, Colonel Rhett. He and his mother, Rebecca, are buried in the Evergreen Slave Cemetery on the Grimball Plantation, where most of the Chavis and Frazier families are buried. His headstone is inscribed with the name Colonel Rhett. His daughter Sarah married Frank (Pipe) Gilliard of Sol Legare.

Leola "Dodie" Lawton Rivers. *Family photograph.*

Rhett lived on the Rivers Plantation and was a farmer, according to my father, Sandy Frazier, Lela (Dodie) Lawton Rivers, Cyrus Frazier and many others. They said that one day in 1939, while Rhett was walking his cow to the pasture, he was leading the cow on a chain when it dragged across a barbwire fence that was touching a live electric wire. Both he and his cow were electrocuted.

Guy Lawton (1880) and his wife Victoria (1886) had three daughters, Heather (1908), Loyola (1913) and Lela "Dodie" (1918); two sons, Guy (1919) and Allison (1921); and a grandson, Liger Watson (1925).

Lela "Dodie" Lawton Rivers (1918) and her husband James Rivers had three sons, Leroy, James and Paul; and three daughters, Blanche, Victoria and Betty Jean.

On October 18, 2005, I interviewed Mrs. "Dodie" Rivers, daughter of Guy Lawton. She said,

Son, let me tell you some things. You were asking me about Bema Rose. Did you know she and my mother Victoria were sisters? Her real name was Rose Washington. She was married to David Cromwell. His nickname was Bema and that is why people called his wife Bema Rose. Their mother was my grandmother, Sarah Washington Fell. I believe Sarah was married twice, possibly three times.

Frazier, my aunt, Bema Rose, was a beautiful light-skinned woman. Her hair was naturally curly and black. It reached down below her shoulders. She had a nice shape and a lot of men admired her. I heard a rumor that a white man liked my aunt but I really don't know. You know all kinds of things were happening on the Hinson, Lawton, Seabrook, Clark, Bee and the Grimball Plantations during the farming years. Just look at the half-white children that were born and raised on James Island. That should tell you something. Frazier, we have come a long way with hard work, prayer and believing in God.

On October 18, 2005, I interviewed Allison Lawton. He said,

Frazier, all of my family is dead now. There are only two of us left—my sister Dodie and me. When I was a young boy growing up, I worked on George Nungezer farm most of my life. That is how I met your daddy, Bosie Frazier.

Boy I tell ya that waz hard time duin them days, wokin in rain, hot sun and in cold weter, plowing, digging ditch, to watering the crops. We pack matoes, cucumbers, eggplant, string beans, collard greens and lota oter crop in crates, bushel baskets and boxes to ship to oter place. I never got married. It just never happened. We make it hur on James Island wid prayer, hard wok and believe in God.

Robert Whaley (1874) and his wife Emma (1875) had one son, Robert Jr. (1902); and nine daughters, Christina (1905), Maggie (1909), Esse (1914), Lena (1911), Henrietta (1918), Emma (1907), Marguerite, Hermenia and Eva.

Joe White (1902) and his wife Rosalee (1904) had four daughters, Rosa Belle (1921), Pearl (1924), Helen (1926) and Mildred (1929); and one son, Joe (1925).

Isiah White (1895) and his wife Celia (1897) had three sons, Gesler (1920), Hezekiah (1922) and Richard (1926); and three daughters, Charlotte (1921), Emma (1928) and Teresa (1924).

Esau Edding (1830) and his wife Bella (1831) had two daughters, Patricia (1857) and Rhina (1869); one son, Prince (1869); and granddaughter Betsy Linning (1855).

Henry Green (1893) and his wife Harriet (1899) had one son, Forest (1921); and one daughter, Alma (1925). Also living with the family was Henry's brother, Henry Leon Green (1909).

William Smashum (1809) and his wife Jane (1813) had three sons, Mingo (1853), Thomas (1854) and William (1859); one daughter, Jenny (1858); and a granddaughter, Jenny (1860).

Thomas Champaign (1901) and his wife Sarah J. (1905) had four daughters, Lucile (1920), Elizabeth (1921), Lillian (1925) and Mary (1927); two sons, Abraham (1926) and James (1929). Thomas's mother, Lydia (1885), also resided with the family.

Nathan Brown (1905) and his wife Henrietta (1910) had one daughter, Sissie (1928); and two sons, John (1929) and William (1921). Living with the family was Nathan's brother, Allan (1895); a sister, Minnie Smalls (1907); and nephews Richard Smalls (1921), Marion Smalls (1926), Henry Smalls (1927) and James Smalls (1929).

The Hinson and Mikell Plantations Owners

JOSEPH B. HINSON (1800) AND his wife Julianna B. (1808) had three daughters, Sarah R. (1833), Martha P. (1835) and Julianna (1841); and two sons, Stiles (1837) and William (1839). Also residing in the home were Starling Hinson (1849) and William Hinson Mikell (1882), but documentation did not specify the relationship.

Joseph M. Mikell (1820) and his wife Conelia (1828) had one daughter, Margaret (1848); and one son Joseph Jr. (1849).

The slave schedule from 1850 to 1860 shows the Mikell and Hinson families owned 166 slaves, including 19 mulattos, during these years.

Slaves and Their Descendants Residing on the Hinson and Mikell Plantations

Peggy Smalls (1840) had two daughters, Lizzie Chisolm (1868) and Rosanna Chisolm (1895). Also living in the household were her mother, Rina Johnson (1815); and three grandsons, Sammy Chisolm, William Chisolm (1892) and Frank Chisolm (1897).

William Brown (1841) and his wife Rosina (1852) had four daughters, Diana (1882), Rebecca (1884), Margaret (1886) and Blossom (1890); and four sons, William (1883), Richard (1882), John (1884) and Samuel (1886).

William Mikell (1868) and his wife Julia (1890) had several family members living with them, including four stepsons, Frank Seabrook, James Seabrook, William Seabrook and Abraham Seabrook. Mr. William Mikell was among the founding fathers of Payne Church.

Robert Smalls (1871) and his wife Nancy (1871) had two sons, Robert Jr. (1892) and George (1899); and two daughters, Hattie (1894) and Sarah (1896). Also living with them were a nephew, Sam Prioleau (1882); and a niece, Christine Prioleau (1888).

Reverend Jack White (1922) was married to Viola Campbell. During my conversations with him, he said,

Son when I was a boy my daddy worked on the Mikell farm and sometimes on the Clark farm for six dollars a week. They grew white potatoes, sweet potatoes and all types of vegetable on the farms.

They raised cows and operated a dairy farm and between the two farms they also raised turkeys. Man it was a shame; because our family lived on the plantation I had to stay home from school to work on the farms while Mr. Mikell's children went to school.

John Bright (1863) and his wife Jane (1864) had two daughters, Mime (1883) and Jane (1893); and four sons, James (1890), Josiah (1887), Edward (1892) and James (1894).

Aaron White (1868) and his wife Hager (1869) raised an adopted son, Sam Pettigrew (1911); two of Hager's sisters, Julia Drayton (1890) and Phyllis Drayton; and a niece (Phyllis's daughter), Laura Bright (1918). Also living with the family was Hager's brother, John Drayton (1876). Mrs. Hager White is listed as one of the founding mothers of Payne RMUE Church, which was founded in 1875 under the Reverend Pappy White.

During an interview with Phyllis Bright Downey (1935), she said,

Frazier, my grandmother's name was Phyllis Drayton. Robert Bright was my grandfather but he and my grandmother Phyllis Drayton were never married. They had one daughter, Laura Bright. Laura had two daughters, Vivian Bright [1936] and I. Hager White, my grandaunt [maternal], raised all of us. People in the community called my mother Laura "Tootsie." She was married to Alfred Richardson.

We were raised in the area known as Society Corner in the Peas Hill Section located off Secessionville Road. My grandaunt, Hager, used to babysit and take care of the children in the community while their parents went to work on the different farms. I remember she wore long dresses. She was a dark-skinned pretty woman with long gray hair.

She used to tell us stories about how she would carry lumber on her shoulder, just as some of the men did in those days. I remember some of the people that lived in our community off Secessionville Road. They were Mr. David [King] Smalls, his wife Rosa and their children, Etta, David, Rosalee and Arolease.

Hager talked about her times working on the Coker farms. She said, "Mr. Coker liked the real 'high yellow' [mulatto] women." I tell you the truth, sometimes the way she talked about Coker, he probably was sweet on her too, but she never admitted this, she would only smile.

My great-granduncle Kit Bright was married to Dafney Mitchell. After the death of Uncle Kit, Dafney married Harry Ford. Grandaunt Hager said that Harry Ford was from Edisto Island. During the late 1800s it took several days to walk from Edisto Island to James Island. He told her how he walked along the edges of riverbanks through canals, dense woods and finally made his way to Stono Road [Riverland Drive] on James Island.

From there he made his way to the Hinson, Mikell and Lawton farms. While working on those farms, he met and married my great-grandaunt, Daphney Bright.

Rose "Bema Rose" Cromwell. *Family photograph.*

Frazier, you mention your grandaunt, Lilly Duxien Todd; she and my grandmother, Phyllis Drayton, were half-sisters.

Harry (Harrison) Ford (1863) and his wife Lucile (1863) had four daughters, Mary (1883), Celia (1886), Anna (1893) and Lydia (1897); and three sons, Edward (1890), Harry Jr. (1892) and Remus (1895). Also living with Harry was his mother-in-law, Isabella Ladson (1822). After the death of Lucile, Harry married his second wife, Daphney.

Harry (Harrison) Ford (1863) and his second wife Daphney (1872) had one son, John (1912); one daughter, Mary (1915); two grandsons, Christopher Bright (1920) and Alfred Bright (1922); one granddaughter, Percilla Bright (1929); and a stepdaughter, Tena Bright (1903).

Ezekiel Fludd (1850) and his wife Hester (1852) had four sons, Ezekiel Jr. (1882), James (1884), Edward (Eddie) (1886) and Paul (1888); four daughters, Kathy (1883), Mary (1884), Molly (1889) and Adeline (1892); and a grandchild, Elvira Mack (1884).

Lazarus Fludd (1850) was married to Hester (1852). Living with them was Lazarus's mother, Mollie (1830). Lazarus Fludd was one of the former slaves who helped carry lumber on his shoulders from the Seabrooks' Boat Landing at Wappoo Creek down a trail some two and a half miles to the corners of Fort Johnson and

Secessionville Road. There the first black Presbyterian Church was built under the leadership of Reverend H. Hunter and completed in 1868.

Edward "Eddie" Fludd (1892) and his wife Betsy (1894) had four daughters, Mary (1911), Ida (1916), Rosa Lee (1918) and Alice (1925); and four sons, Mikell (1920), Benjamin (1922), John (1924) and Edward (1928).

Kit Cromwell (1818) and his wife Jane (1821) had three sons, Richard (1856), Kit (1843) and Ronnie (1845); and three daughters, Miley (1850), Sarah (1867) and Betsy (1869).

Alfred (Hog) Cromwell (1868) and his wife Janie had four sons, Alfred, John Henry, Eugene and Jackie; and two daughters, Janie and Beatrice.

David (Bema) Cromwell Sr. (1882) and his wife Rose (1892) had one daughter, Maybell (1913–2003); and one son, Buster (1929). Rose was called Bema Rose because her husband's nickname was Bema. There were several women in the community named Rose, so the people called her Bema Rose to identify her from the other Roses. Rose was a very attractive woman; she was known for her shapely body and her long black natural curly hair that reached below her shoulders. She was said to have been an affectionate and caring person with a pleasant attitude. It was said that she was admired by many men in the community, including the white men working on the plantations.

David (Buster) Cromwell (1929) and his wife Dorothy (1931) had four sons, David, Paul, Ronald and Francis; and two daughters, Rose Marie and Althea.

David was affectionately called Buster by people in the community. According to his wife, he worked on the Hinson and Nungezer farms for several years and was employed by one of the local ice companies in Charleston for over twenty years before he retired. After his retirement, Buster had a small farm of his own that he enjoyed gardening until he was unable to work in it. I remember him as a quiet and humble man who was easy to talk with. He was a member of St. James Presbyterian Church.

Edison Edding (1830) and his wife Bella (1831) had two daughters, Tena (1857) and Rhina (1869); and a son, James (1869). Rhina and James were twins. Also living with the family was Betsy Lining (1855).

Simeon Pinckney (1826–1921) and his wife Isabelle (1828) had one son, Daniel McLeod (1848). Isabelle and Daniel were mulattos, according to oral history by slaves and their descendants and as told to me by Aida Moore, Harry Urie and Cyrus Frazier. In researching this material, information revealed that Isabelle was the daughter of a slave woman fathered by a plantation owner. She was given to Mr. McLeod during her young age to be a companion to young Annie McLeod.

Isabelle married Simeon Pinckney, a freedman who came to James Island from the Manning, South Carolina, area. Records reveal that he originally came to this country from Spain. According to the census, Isabelle had one son, whom she named Daniel McLeod, a stepson of Simeon. According to oral history and an article written about her life, on her death bed in 1935, Annie McLeod Frampton asked for her lifelong friend and former slave Isabelle, saying, "I hope to see her in heaven." There are no known records as to what happened to

Isabelle Pinckney. *Family photograph.*

Daniel McLeod, son of Isabelle. However, according to oral history passed down by slaves, Daniel McLeod was murdered by a white man after they discovered that he was a black man having an affair with a white woman.

Simeon Pinckney (1826) and his wife Phyllis (1859) had three sons, Ellis (1887), Simeon Jr. (1889) and Matthew (1895); and a granddaughter, Diana Mary Ford (1888), according to the 1900 census report.

However, descendants of Simeon Pinckney, Julius (Steven) Brown and several other family members said that Simeon never married a second wife and none of the children listed by Phyllis were fathered by Simeon. A great-great-grandson, Julius Brown, said Simeon, as a freeman, bought twenty acres of land on Fort Johnson Road where he and many descendants still reside. The descendants of Simeon filed a lawsuit in probate court against the estate that is still pending as of this writing. Records revealed he died in 1921, leaving his wife Isabelle a widow.

Ellis Pinckney (1887) and his wife Hattie (1890) had two daughters, Elouise Pinckney Harris (1915–2004) and Isadora Pinckney. During an interview, Mrs. Elouise Pinckney Harris said,

> *Frazier, I also had two brothers, Josiah Pinckney and Julius Pinckney. My granddaddy, Simeon, came to James Island from I believe Manning, South Carolina. He met Grandma Phyllis here on James Island and they got married. Simeon came here a freedman and bought this property here on Fort Johnson Road during slavery and it has been in the family ever since.*
>
> *I went to Three Trees School on the Clark Plantation just off Fort Johnson Road. The school was a three-room board building painted red. It was built high up off the ground. Aida White, her sister Isadora White and me went to school there together. My family was very blessed they were not slaves and I did not have to work on the farm like my friend Aida and many others did. Sometimes I did go on the farms to earn extra money for personal uses.*
>
> *Frazier, my daddy, Ellis Pinckney, worked at the quarantine stations for the government at the end of Fort Johnson Road on James Island. This was where the boats came to the island. The people who were sick had to be quarantined and fumigated. Some had smallpox and others were sick with malaria and other types of diseases. Many died during those years.*
>
> *Daddy slept at work and came home twice a week. We used to be able to look out of our window and see the Atlantic Ocean before the woods and bushes grew up around here. After I came of age, I moved to New York and got married, but after the death of my husband I came back home to stay.*

Paul Williams (1882) and his wife Molly (1885) had five sons, Paul Jr. (1913), John (1917), Franklin (1916), J. (1915) and Eddie; and six daughters, Molly (1902), Sarah (1911), Gertie (1918), Gertrude (1916), Rosa Lee (1923) and Hattie (1925).

John White (1900) and his wife Nancy (1905) had two daughters, Erma (1920) and Dorothy (1928); and two sons, Jack (1922) and Johnnie (1925).

Willoughby Geddes (1833) was a widower. He had two sons, General (1862) and Matthew (1866); and two daughters, Ida (1867) and Jane.

Henry Archer (1840) and his wife Cynthia (1845) had four sons, Daniel (1863), Edward (1866), Joe (1872) and Henry, all mulattos.

Woodland Riley (1820) and his wife Eliza (1830) had two daughters, Livinia (1850) and Hannah (1855); and two sons, Paul (1857) and Benjamin Rivers (1858). Paul Riley (1857) was married to Hester Riley (1860).

Squire Haley (1829) and his wife Maria (1833) had two daughters, Isabella (1868) and Emily (1869).

THE ROYALL PLANTATION OWNERS

Wᴵᴸᴸᴵᴬᴹ Rᴏʏᴀʟ (1798) ᴀɴᴅ ʜɪs wife Mary (1803) had three sons, John B. (1837), Basile (1839) and Croskey (1841); and one daughter, Catharine (1843). Croskey Royall (1798) and his wife Valeria (1818) had one daughter, Martha (1835); and two sons, James P. (1840) and Edward D. (1849).

The slave schedule from 1850 to 1860 shows the Royall family owned ten slaves during this period.

THE MELLECHAMP
PLANTATION OWNERS

S TILE MELLECHAMP (1785) AND HIS wife Margaret (1807) had three daughters, Jane (1826), Martha (1828) and Sarah Ann (1831); and three sons, William A. (1833), Joseph (1836) and Stile (1840).

The slave schedule of 1850 shows the Mellechamp family owned fifty-seven slaves at that time.

THE LEBBY PLANTATION OWNERS

Robert Lebby Jr. (1854) and his wife Lillie (1854) had four daughters, Mary L. (1884), Lilly B. (1885), Kate G. (1895) and Cecile J. (1888); and two sons, L. Lee (1886) and Robert (1889).

The slave schedule from 1850 to 1860 shows the Lebby family owned twenty-two slaves during that period.

THE HILL PLANTATION OWNERS

JOSEPH HILL (1823) AND HIS wife Adele (1827) had two sons, William B. (1846) and George W. (1848).
The slave schedule from 1850 to 1860 shows the Hill family owned twelve slaves during that period.

NUNGEZER FARM FROM THE 1920S THROUGH THE 1960S

GEORGE NUNGEZER (1890) AND HIS wife Eva M. Nungezer (1907) had one son, George Jr. (1933). Nungezer leased and farmed the property in the Whitehouse area off Fort Johnson Road from the 1920s through the late 1950s. George Nungezer Jr. was killed by a Civil War cannonball that he was beating with a hammer in 1948.

THE CHANGING TIMES

FOLLOWING THE SIGNING OF THE Emancipation Proclamation and at the end of the War Between the States, the Freedmen's Bureau was set up on the McLeod Plantation. The government divided the deserted lands along the Sea Islands, and the head of each slave's family was to be given forty acres and a mule. Dozens of slave families did receive land around the Sea Island area. Around the mid-1800s, 15 to 20 percent of the land in the Sea Island area was owned by blacks.

However, by 1880, most of the land awarded to blacks was taken and returned to its original white plantation owners. In the mid-1800s and early 1900s, blacks on James Island began having a little leeway in reference to managing their lives. The State of South Carolina allowed blacks to form an all-black militia force on James Island. This granted them the authority to arm themselves and arrest and control unruly blacks. They were known as the "Hunter Volunteers."

The headquarters' building for the militia was located at the intersection of Riverland Drive and Grimball Road where the Riverside Lodge Hall building is today. It was near the Civil War battery that ran through the Dill Plantation, across the road from Charles Whaley's house. Some of its members included Isaac Fergerson (1849), captain in charge of the unit; Henry Green, the sergeant and second in command; Amos Watson (1848); Thomas Middleton (1858); Charles Knightly (1820); and Julius Richardson (1876).

Most blacks were Republicans in 1876. At the first Republican convention held on James Island on the issue of allowing blacks to vote, there was trouble at the poll. A black woman, Maria (Knight) Knightly (1822), was shot in the jaw by Sergeant Green, a member of the militia who was said to have been intoxicated. He turned himself into authorities; the shooting was ruled an accident and the charge was dismissed. Amos Watson (1848) and Charles (Knight) Knightly (1822) were the first two known black Democratic registered voters on James Island.

Over the years, I have had numerous conversations with my father, Frank Deleston, Paul Chisolm and many of the older men and women in the community concerning the history of James Island. During one of these conversations, Frank Deleston said, "Son, my Pa told me there were only four free slaves on

James Island during slavery that he knew: James Prioleau, Paul Chavis, Sammy Dixon and Simeon Pinckney."

Sammy Dixon, according to paper and deed, is Samson Duxien of Riverland Drive. Records showed that he purchased twenty acres of land from Joseph and Regina Dill for $400 in 1879. This property sits next to King Solomon Lodge Hall.

As cousin Frank took a puff off his pipe while smoking he said, "My Pa, Joseph Deleston, your great-grandpa Cyrus Frazier, Paul Chavis and many of the other slaves tended the white James Island Presbyterian Church on Fort Johnson Road. When I was a boy, people called it Quarantine Road. The slaves sat upstairs during worship service and the white people sat downstairs."

Session records from the James Island Presbyterian Church for the years 1833 to 1845 show that there were 34 white communicants, 1 freedman and 153 slaves that attended church. Only the baptismal names of the slaves were used and they were listed under the names of their plantation owners.

In 1865, according to the minutes from the white Presbyterian church, the church was destroyed by a fire started in a nearby field by Confederate soldiers. The members were left without a place to worship; white communicants held worship service at the home of one of its members, Mr. Ephraim Clark, a plantation and slave owner.

The black members congregated under a large oak tree at the intersection of Quarantine Road (Fort Johnson Road) and old Savannah Road (Secessionville Road). The site was where the first black St. James Presbyterian Church was built, the same site where St. James Presbyterian Church stands today. The minutes from the white James Island Presbyterian Church corroborate and substantiate these events.

Following the signing of the Emancipation Proclamation, in 1866, Reverend H. Hampleton Hunter, a freedman from the Northern Presbyterian church, came to work with the newly freed people. He organized and built the first St. James Presbyterian Church; and in 1867, Reverend Hunter organized the first Mission School under the umbrella of the St. James Presbyterian Church using the church as a school.

It was there that the recently freed slaves were taught to read and write. According to Cousin Frank Deleston, he said, "Me, Paul Chisolm, Abraham Brown, James [Brooks] Williams, Sandy Frazier Sr., Charles Whaley and some I don't remember tended the school." The Mission School was the first in Charleston County to teach blacks to read and write.

Frank Deleston became an elder and the clerk of sessions for the church for several years, even during my tenure as a Sunday school student. Session minutes from the white James Island Presbyterian Church dated February 17, 1867, state that "the colored portion of the former [interracial] congregation had, previous to this, been entirely wrestled away from us, by emissaries of the Northern Church, and at this time worshiped to themselves."

For January 1, 1868, the minutes from the St. James Presbyterian Church state, "the Atlantic Presbytery was officially established, under the action of

Memorial dedicated to the founder and teachers of St. James Parochial School. *Family photograph.*

the Synod of Baltimore. There were six founders The Reverend H. Hampleton Hunter, Jonathon Gibbs, Ishmael Moultrie, William T. Smith [all black] and William T. Carr and Matthew R. Miller [both white]."

The committee on freedmen reported to the general assembly that St. James Presbyterian Church was completed at a cost of $800. It had a membership of four hundred communicants, eighty Sunday school students and eighty-nine pupils in its Mission School.

Reverend Hunter served the St. James Presbyterian Church as it pastor and headmaster of the Mission School from 1867 until his death on October 6, 1893. Records indicated that he served with distinction during his tenure. After Reverend Hunter's death, several ministers served as acticing pastors for the church until a permanent replacement could be found. These ministers included the Reverend Adam Fraye, John Miller, Joseph Pearson and Reverend C.H. Uggams. The Mission School remained closed until Reverend Marion Sanders received the call to become both the pastor of the church and headmaster of the school.

A memorial monument stands at the corner of Secessionville and Fort Johnson Road, on the church property in memory of Reverend H.H. Hunter, Reverend Marion, Mrs. Ona Belle Sanders, and the schoolteachers of St. James

St. James Presbyterian Church after it was rebuilt in 1906. *Courtesy of St. James Presbyterian Church Archives.*

Parochial School. This monument was erected as the result of a fundraising drive conducted by some of the former student body of St. James Parochial School and its president, Eugene Frazier, in 2003.

In 1923, fresh out of the seminary, Reverend Marion A. Sanders (1888) and his wife, Ona Belle (1898), natives of Charlotte, North Carolina, at the urging of one of the elders accepted the call as pastor of St. James Presbyterian Church on James Island. The young preacher saw the need and immediately reopened the Mission School. He was the headmaster and teacher. His wife was also a teacher and an administrator.

The people were poor and in need of help and, through the urging of Reverend Sanders, the Board of National Mission in New York began sending boxes of clothing to be distributed to the needy on the island regardless of their religious affiliation or which school they attended.

The children learned early in their lives what it meant by, "It takes a village to raise a child." Any adult that lived in the community had the authority to discipline them with what they deemed appropriate, such as a belt or a piece of branch broken from a tree limb, when a child misbehaved. Mrs. Ethel Frazier Campbell said,

Eugene, when Reverend and Mrs. Sanders re-opened the Mission School in 1923, I was in the very first class. Among my classmates were Ethel Richardson Turner

Reverend Sanders, *right*, and Mrs. Sanders, *far left*, along with the students of St. James Parochial School in the front of the school. Ethel Campbell, the author's aunt, is the first student on the right in the middle row. (1923–24). *Courtesy of St. James Presbyterian Church Archives.*

and Mary Seabrook Goss. Classes were taught in the church. Sometime during 1924, Reverend Sanders, with the blessing of the church officers, purchased a three-room board house across Fort Johnson Road. They placed it on rollers and rolled it on the church's property.

Although the building was old and dilapidated looking it had two windows in the front with windowpanes and a rear door made of a board that opened outward. The men of the church got together and repaired and painted the building. We were glad to have our own schoolhouse. In 1930, Reverend Sanders and his wife Ona Belle instituted the May Day Festival that became poplar around the entire Sea Island area, including Beaufort, South Carolina, and Savannah, Georgia.

In the late 1890s, Charleston County opened four satellite grade schools for blacks on James Island. One was called Cut Bridge School. It was located on Riverland Drive and stood in a lowland area next to the small canal that the James Island County Park now occupies. Students that attended school there were oftentimes wet in classes due to the crossing of the canal. This two-room board building accommodated the students from the Dill Plantation, which included the Cut Bridge area.

The second school was called Three Trees. It was also a two-room board building. It was located on Fort Johnson Road at the east end of the island. This school accommodated all students in the Fort Johnson area on the island. The South Carolina Electric and Gas Company now has a power plant in that location. The third school was called Society Corner, a two-room board building; it was located on Secessionville Road, next to Westchester subdivision, by the tall Civil War battery that stretched across the island. The school building is now part of a house at number 1395 Secessionville Road. Society Corner accommodated the students on the Grimball Plantation area. The fourth school was called Patrick. It was in a two-room board building located on Sol Legare Road. It accommodated those students that lived in that area. The Sol Legare Community Center now occupies this location. All other students that lived on James Island regardless of locations could attend the Mission School, also known as St. James Parochial School, if they chose to.

In 1941, I started attending St. James Parochial School under Reverend Marion Sanders. There were five teachers besides him. The teachers for grades first through eighth included Mrs. Ona Belle Sanders, Mrs. Martha R. Gladden, Mr. Adam Davis, Mrs. Leola W. Whaley, Mrs. Louise Metz, Mrs. Lula William and Ms. Maggie Belle Sanders. There were several substitute teachers that helped out at the school when they were needed.

Mr. Adam Davis and Fred Gibbs were the athletic directors and Mrs. Cecile Richardson and Mrs. Louise Williams were the dietitians. The building was a three-room board building with a kitchen. Reverend Sanders initiated a lunch program in the school. Each student received a cup of hot soup and a slice of bread for ten cents per day. The students who were unable to pay received free lunch. When I started attending St. James Parochial School in 1941, the May Day Festival was going strong and continued throughout the 1960s and 1970s in many areas, from James Island to Johns Island and most of the Sea Island areas. Even the Charleston and Beaufort areas instituted the program. Every year since my leaving St. James Parochial School, the festival continued to grow larger on James Island. Over four hundred people would participate in the parade and functions held on the church's property.

The majority of the boys in the community between the ages of seven to fifteen had many chores assigned to do at home. Most parents were farmers and laborers; my father rented several acres of land to farm next to our property from Raymond Grimball of the Grimball Plantation.

In the morning before sunrise, I had to water the mule and cow and take them out in the field to graze and chop firewood before going to school. At the end of the school day, my first cousin, Thomas Smalls (who was raised by my grandmother) and I had to plow and cultivate the farms. These chores lasted five and a half days a week; this was standard procedure for most boys of our age in the community. Very few blacks had electricity during this time; we studied our school lessons at night by using kerosene lamps.

I recall one evening, Thomas and I were plowing a field on the farm located about a thousand yards behind our house near some woods. Approximately fifty yards inside the woods was a moonshine whiskey still. It belonged to one of the men in the community.

Thomas and I went to the still; there was corn mash inside a fifty-five-gallon drum barrel that had ferment on the top and was ready to be manufactured into whiskey. We took a quart jar and filled it with the ferment on top of the barrel; Thomas and I took turns drinking until we got intoxicated. We did not realize that it was getting dark so we kept on plowing.

My father came down to see why we were still plowing as by that time we should have quit and watered the mule long before. As he talked with us, he smelled the odor and realized that we were intoxicated. It would be the first and last time this happened because of the wide leather belt he used on us. I could not sit down that night or the next day without placing something soft under my bottom.

Between 1948 and 1950, at the end of each school day, I would meet my father in the Crescent subdivision. He had quit working on the Nungezer farm and was doing landscaping work. The Crescent was and still is located north of the Wappoo Bridge on the east side of Folly Road headed north toward the city of Charleston.

I recall several white families living in the Crescent that my father worked for during the 1940s and continuing throughout the 1960s: Mr. and Mrs. Thomas Liddy, John and Beverly McGee, Hall and Peggy McGee, Dr. John and Mrs. Mood, Mr. Harold A. Petit (president of SCE&G Company) were some of them.

Although segregation was rigidly enforced during those years and everywhere one would look there were signs saying colored and white, the Liddys, Moods and McGees treated my father and I with dignity and respect. In fact when we worked for the Liddys and Moods, we were allowed to sit at their kitchen table and eat our lunch.

During the time I attended Burke High School, I helped my father with his landscaping work after school. The Liddys had two daughters, Rita (Peatsie) Liddy (who years later would become the wife of Senator Ernest Fritz Holling) and Kay Liddy Baldwin. I would never forget this family for the loyalty, help and affection shown by them to my family during those difficult years.

Folly Road was the only paved road on James Island during the 1930s. All other road surfaces were dirt; Grimball Road, as all other secondary roads on the island, was one lane. Whenever it rained, the road surface became muddy. Only one car was able to pass as the second car had to wait. Sometimes it was miserable walking to and from school in the rain and through the mud.

Where my family lived on Grimball Road, we were a little more fortunate than many others. Other children had to walk as much as five miles. Our house was two and a half miles from the St. James Parochial School on Fort Johnson Road at Secessionville Road. Many days, the white students passed on their school buses while we walked. Muddy water from the large school bus tires would splash on us. They would laugh, calling us "niggers," "poor niggers." This was an accepted way of life during those years; besides, there was nothing anyone could do about the situation.

During those turbulent years in the 1920s throughout the 1950s, the Charleston County Public Works Department used black men on the chain gang to clean ditches and drainage by the roadways. Most of the time two white men guarded the prisoners with shotguns while they worked. The men had a chain hooked to a metal ball around their ankle that would make it difficult to escape; they wore black-and-white pinstriped uniforms during this period.

I remember the ditches being at least 3½ feet wide and up to 4 feet deep in certain areas. The County Public Works Department used a road scraper or tractor to keep the one-lane road clean. Cousin Louis Gladden and Isaac Kinlock would sometime drive the tractor to scrape the one-lane road. The ditches were kept clean by the black convicts on the chain gang with bush knives, forks and shovels.

When it rained, the ditches would get full with rainwater. During the summer months, the children in the community would jump into the ditch to swim. During one of the swims, Thomas and I had an encounter with a water moccasin snake lurking in the ditch. It did not take long to heed our parents' stern warning to stay out of the ditches.

During harvest time, my mother would take the vegetables, including okra, tomatoes, green beans, squash, corns and cucumbers, to the city market in downtown Charleston to sell. She would ride with one of the farmers who was fortunate enough to own a truck during those trying times. Charles Whaley and Enoch Whaley of the Grimballs' Plantation and James Bennett (Son Bennett) of the Dill Plantation were some of the men who owned those little Ford trucks.

The money my mother made from selling the vegetables was used to help my father buy the bare necessities for our survival. Those were hard times for our family and the majority of blacks on the island. By this time, I had five sisters. There were times when my mother had to wash the same clothes every night for us to wear to school the next day.

My father and mother were determined that all of us would get an education no matter what sacrifices they had to make. My father told me he did not want me to suffer as he did; working from sunup to sundown sometimes sixteen hours a day earning barely enough money for our family's survival. He said that education, hard work with a strong determination and a spiritual background believing in God would be the answer for the survival of black people.

I recall times when I was ten years old; my father would leave home going to work sick, with toothaches, swollen jaw and back pain. My mother would look at him with a sad expression and say, "Boise, please go to the doctor"; but he would say, "Sis, we have no money." During this time, the majority of the people on the island were in the same predicament as we were.

Between 1942, and 1947, every Saturday my paternal grandmother, Mary Chavis Frazier, grandaunt Irene Chavis Gilliard, Mamie Gladden, Rebecca

Chisolm and other farmers' wives would take their vegetables to sell in the streets of Charleston. Each had their pushcart mounted on two wheels. It was large enough to hold several bushels of different types of vegetables.

I was responsible for pushing my grandmother's cart while Thomas pushed the cart of our grandaunt, Irene Chavis Gilliard. Sometimes we would alternate. Clarence Gibbs pushed the cart of his grandmother, Mamie Gladden, and Benjamin Smith pushed the cart of his grandmother, Rebecca Chisolm. As we pushed the vegetable carts throughout the Charleston peninsula, the women would chant, "I got your okra, tomatoes, corns, string beans, turnip, squash and collard greens. Come and get it!"

They would repeat this chant most of the day until all of the vegetables were sold. I recall one Saturday in 1944; a city policeman stopped my grandmother and me on Spring Street near President. The police officer asked my grandma, "Annie, do you have a peddler license?" She replied, "No sur."

The officer said, "You better go down to the station house and get one. Let the little nigger boy stay with your cart till you get back." My grandmother was smoking her pipe at the time. As she took the pipe out of her mouth and told the policemen, "Yes sur," I could see the hurt in her eye as she told me she would be right back. I never did forget that incident.

As a young boy, I began to realize that something was awfully wrong with the way black people were being treated. We had to walk to school while whites rode buses, we had to stand on public transportation and allow white people to sit. We could not sit and eat in public restaurants. My father tried to explain to me what segregation meant. He said, "There were some white people that would resort to violence rather than see the races mixed." As I got older, I understood what he meant.

During this era, there were several corner grocery stores on James Island. One was located at the intersection of Folly Road and Sol Legare Road. Another was located at the corner of Folly Road and Battery Island Drive; another was located at the corner of Grimball Road and Folly Road. There was another at the corner of Fort Johnson and Secessionville Roads.

All of these small grocery stores had a gas tank that was equipped with a hand crank to pump gas into cars and a kerosene oil drum for the people who needed oil. The only gas station on the island that performed any type of maintenance on cars or trucks was located at the corner of Maybank Highway and Folly Road, and was operated by Tommy Welch.

In addition to my chores at home, I accompanied my mother and sisters on farms to help our father earn money to pay expenses. Park Mikell, who was managing Dill Plantation during the 1930s through 1960s, had several satellite farm locations. The first location was at the intersection of Folly Road and Riverland Drive where the Food Lion and the Bank of America now stand. This was one of the locations where green beans, Irish potatoes, corn and tomatoes were harvested.

The second location was at the intersection of Folly Road and Central Park Road, where the United States Post Office and the James Island Theater now stand. The third location was on Riverland Drive across from Fergerson Village. The fourth location was in the area of Turkey Pen where my grandfather and other slaves used to live and is now occupied by Meridian Home Complex.

The fifth location was in the area surrounding the Dill Plantation house on the Stono River and Riverland Drive next to the slave cemetery. Finally the sixth location was in the area in front of the tall battery near the canal and Riverland Drive.

The farmer paid twenty-five cents per bushel to pick green beans and ten cents for a hundred-pound bag of potatoes. In 1949, the price was raised to fifty cents per bushel for string beans, and twenty-five cents for a two-hundred-pound bag of potatoes. I recall times my mother, four sisters and I worked the entire day picking string beans and earned eight dollars; this was an injustice of the worst kind.

I remember Nay Joe Deleston, Sanders Smalls, Herman Goss, Alonzo Moore, Albert Smalls and many more all worked for Park Mikell. As the workers waited for them to plow the fields with the tractor, turning up the soil, the potatoes would be picked up, placed in buckets and then dumped into hundred-pound bags until they were filled.

Trucks would be driven through the fields, with the men loading the potatoes, taking them to the market. Jeffery Lemon, or "Mr. Jeffery" as he was affectionately called, was the foreman on the Dill farm during this era; he was entrusted with the task of paying the workers their wages.

In 1949, several classmates and I completed eighth grade at St. James Parochial School on James Island. Prior to this time, there were no high schools on James Island for blacks. The black students who wanted to obtain a high school education had to furnish their own transportation to Burke or Avery High School in the city of Charleston. Most of them walked to Charleston.

During the years 1949 to 1950, the State Department of Transportation began furnishing school buses to transport black students to high school in Charleston. I attributed this move by the State Department of Transportation as a direct result of the petition filed by Mr. Harry Briggs on behalf of his son challenging school segregation in the U.S. District Court in 1948.

There were two public transportation companies in the Metropolitan Charleston area: the South Carolina Electric and Gas Company buses and the Folly Beach Greyline Bus.

Upon entering either of the public transportation buses, blacks had to sit from the rear toward the front and the whites from the front toward the rear. If all seats were full and a white person entered the bus, the black passenger sitting nearest the front had to stand, allowing the white person to sit.

I still remember that hot summer day in 1948; I caught the Folly Beach Greyline Bus at the intersection of Folly Road and Grimball Road. I was headed to the Crescent to meet my father to do some landscaping work. As I boarded the bus, all seats were full. It was standing room only.

The bus made a stop at Dr. Ellis Bridge (Ellis Creek Bridge) on Folly Road across the road from where the Harris Teeter is now located and the entrance to Lowes

Eugene Frazier, first platoon sergeant. *Family photograph.*

Reverend Cornelius Campbell, former pastor of St. James Presbyterian Church. *Family photograph.*

Lumber Company. A white teenage girl came aboard the bus. The driver told the black woman sitting nearest the front that she had to stand and let the girl sit down.

Although I was young, I could still see the expression today on her face when she relinquished her seat. She stood up looking down at the floor of the bus. She appeared to be weeping but no tears were coming. She was saying, "This is not right! God knows this is not right, one day God going to fix this." I felt her pain that day as though it was happening to me. All public facilities such as restaurants, hotels and movies were off limits to blacks unless they worked there. I recall there were a couple of places in Charleston that would serve blacks, provided they stood outside. The food was handed out to them.

The Greyhound Bus Station on Society Street and the Piggy Park Drive-in on Rutledge Avenue were two of the places where blacks could not go inside, but could be served through the window.

After leaving Burke High School, I enlisted in the United States Army. I served a total of six years and was honorably discharged in 1959 as a sergeant.

I was hired by Chief Silas Welch as the fifth black police officer in the Charleston County Police Department. It would later become the Charleston County Sheriff's Department.

In 1963, Federal District Judge J. Robert Martin ruled in the case *Millicent E. Brown vs. School Board District 20* that black children should be allowed to attend any school in the district. Following this ruling, Millicent Brown, daughter of J. Arthur Brown, local businessman, president of the local branch of the NAACP and a resident of James Island, would become the first black person enrolled in the then all-white Rivers High School.

In 1969, Reverend Cornelius L. Campbell Jr. accepted the "call" as pastor for St. James Presbyterian Church. Reverend Campbell was a staunch supporter and leader of African Americans on James Island during the school integration crisis. Under Reverend Campbell's leadership, the congregation was sucessful in reference to its building fund campaign and construction of the present church at Fort Johnson and Secessionville Road.

Reverend Dr. Charles Heyward and his wife, Carolyn Heyward, took over as pastor and assistant pastor after much searching and deliberation for a qualified candidate to replace Reverend Campbell. Reverend Heyward assumed his duties in May 1996 to become the sixth pastor of St. James Presbyterian Church; he continues to advance the spiritual growth of St. James Presbyterian Church.

During the mid-1950s through 1960s, Dr. Martin Luther King Jr. was appearing all over the country seeking social changes and equal justice for blacks. In 1967, J. Arthur Brown, the civil rights activist and president of the local NAACP, made a request to Charleston County Council for protection for Dr. King during a speaking engagement at Charleston County Hall.

Chief Silas Welch, a native of James Island, assigned Detective James L. Mikell, Detective George Gathers and me to escort Dr. King from the Charleston Municipal Airport to a speaking engagement at Charleston County Hall on King Street and to provide security for him until he left Charleston.

Chief Welch told us if any harm came to Dr. King while he was in Charleston, that we would be fired. We assured the chief that no harm would come to Dr. King while he was with us in Charleston. Although segregation was still being enforced between the races, I considered Chief Silas Welch a man of great strength and wisdom. He was a decent and ethical man during those trying times.

Dr. King would be assassinated the following year in April of 1968, in Tennessee.

In Conclusion

As I reflect back to the time when blacks first arrived here as slaves from Africa and other parts of the world, I cannot help but think about the progress we have made. We have achieved every reachable goal that the white man would allow us, from slavery, where we were forbidden to read and write, to sharecropping and farming. African Americans have traveled the road of despair through the woods, footpaths and dirt trails and have seen this island transformed from a wilderness to part of a modern city.

African Americans born and raised on James Island have become medical doctors, nurses, police officers, lawyers, CIA operatives, secret service officers, Hall of Fame golfers and have obtained their PhDs in many different fields. Still many others have left and gone to other states and were elected to many high offices.

Victor Hill. *Family photograph.*

In Conclusion

Victor Hill, formerly of James Island, became the first black sheriff in the history of Clayton County, Georgia, in 2005. He left the Charleston County Sheriff's Office in 1991 after he was terminated because of what he labeled the department's racist policy.

I believe the time is long overdue for South Carolina, Charleston in particular, to live up to the constitution that the forefathers crafted this country after: that all men were created equal. In following the philosophy of Dr. King, I hope the day will soon come where my children and grandchildren will be judged on their qualifications and not the color of their skin here in Charleston.

GLOSSARY

afa—after
ain't—am not
ax—ask
bog—stuck
bubber—brother
buckra—derogatory term for a white person
cath—caught
certun—certain
chillin—children
chimmy—chimney
chunk—throw
cun—cousin
cuton—cotton
cutting—cotton
da—the or this
dat—that
daz—days
ded—died or dead
dem—the or them
deth—death
dey—they, their or sometimes the
duin—during
eart—earth
em—them
everting—everything
fine—find
ford—afford

fore—before
fretting—irritated
fron—from
fur—far
gab—grabbed
geter—gather or harvest
gimmie—give me
gu—got
har—hear
heals—healed
high yellow—lighter skinned or mulatto
hoss—horse
hur—her
hut—hurt or injured
juke joint—night club
liver—deliver
loss—lost
Massa—Master
matos—tomatoes
member—remember
mon—men or man
mont—month
mout—mouth
notting—nothing
nuff—enough
omen—women
oter—other
oversey—overseer

GLOSSARY

rond—around
roun—wrong
Satday—Saturday
scabs—scars
scrapin—scrapping
shitten—mean, angry
spec—expect
stom—storm
suchin—searching
sur—sir
ta—to
tart—start
tater—potato
tay—stay
teaf—steal
tention—attention
tight—intoxicated or drunk
ting—thing
tink—think or thought
tron—strong
tu—to
tuk—took
tunin—turning
un—and or an
usta—used to
uta—used to

wanna—want to
waz—was or were
wen—when
weter—whether
wha—what
wid—would or with
wod—word
wok—work
wokers—workers
wold—world
yea—years
yu—you
youn—young

ABOUT THE AUTHOR

EUGENE FRAZIER SR. IS A retired lieutenant with the Charleston County Sheriff's Department. He is married to Francis E. Frazier and they have three children and six grandchildren. He is a lifelong resident of James Island and is an active member of St. James Presbyterian Church. He enjoys a fulfilling life surrounded by his family and friends.

Visit us at
www.historypress.net

www.ingramcontent.com/pod-product-compliance
Lightning Source LLC
Chambersburg PA
CBHW081944060525
26242CB00043B/165